Around-Town
CYCLING

Around-Town CYCLING

by DONALD PRUDEN

Published by
World Publications

Contents

Introduction

Ecology, economics, health, fat removal—phooey! All fallacies of the adult delusion that one must have a serious reason for doing anything at all once one is past the age of 18. Why can't fun and function go together? The automobile is about as much fun as an elevator, to the addicted cyclist. The bicycle becomes, on the other hand, an increasingly fertile playground for the human forces of self-expression and creative whim. Society allows you to forget your age on a bicycle, so why not cop a few thrills right under its noses?

People's motives for buying bicycles are often scholarly and grim—heart attack prevention, rising gas prices, ecology, etc. But once you're hooked, you'll need no such intellectual props. Unfortunately, explaining why cycling is a satisfying thing to do in itself is a little like trying to explain ice cream to a person who's never seen it. James Carson's article will give you a better taste of short-distance cycling than any amount of artificial reconstruction of its flavors. (See page 20.)

The goal of *Around-Town Cycling* is to develop minimal skills of technique and maintenance to make cycling enjoyable, efficient and to convince you that it's really a sane and safe thing to do in traffic. If you're a rider of youthful or middle years, I hope at least to turn you into an old rider by inclination.

No attempt has been made to make this one of the "complete" works on cycling. Those who've used the bicycle as transportation for years will probably not find this book terribly enlightening. It is mainly a sharing of my experiences and readings with those who'll be "pioneering"—leaving the car at home more and more frequently because they're finding it a lot less hassle and a lot more fun to ride.

Utility cycling—riding a bike because it's practical—leads to the harder stuff; not because of some bitter-sweet masochistic incentive, but because riding regularly taps unique, long-lost body-mind pleasures.   It's addictive.   (Dan Burden photo).

Dog attacks, collisions, a physical assault and thousands of miles shared with a friend have prepared me, I think, to offer advice to brother and sister cyclists of less experience. Good times with my students at the Milne School, adult education classes, workshops and summer rec programs all helped develop the contents of "Around-Town Cycling." One of the beauties of teaching is that the teacher often learns as much as he imparts.

Chapter 1

Swearing Off Cars

I am constantly asked, "Isn't cycling dangerous? What about all those trucks?" Have you ever looked into the fatality rate from falling in the shower or from eating a meal? As for trucks, you are probably. in far greater danger from your neighbor in the VW than from the biggest rig on the road. Given my druthers, I'll share the roadway with a trucker anyday. That rig may seem terrifying but there is a true professional at the wheel. Can you say the same for your neighbor? Do you know any alcoholic truck drivers?

Just what is "safe"?

On a typical one-way trip to work I am passed by an average of 170 other vehicles. In over 1200 trips I have had one mishap, and that was when a car failed to yield at a stop sign. One other accident was a collision with a dog. In those 1200 trips I have been passed by over 200,000 vehicles, crossed 122,400 intersections and 250,000 driveways, and passed more than 270,000 parked cars. In that time I have been chased by at least 5,000 dogs.

Contrary to appearances, traffic is *not* random! There is considerable order to it and traffic laws are one of the means agreed upon to maintain that order. Accidents happen when one or more of the drivers or riders involved has done something to increase the randomness of the traffic system.

With 100,000,000 bicycles known to be owned in the United States, there were about 1,100 fatalities in 1974. Most of these involved riders under 16 years old. *There's* a high entropy group if there ever was one! Ten times as many pedestrians were killed in the same period, and over 50 times as many died in cars. In at least half of those cases—over 25,000—alcohol was a known factor.

Is riding a bicycle dangerous? Well, twice as many died in 1974 choking on a poorly-swallowed bit of food. Have you considered not eating? More people eat than ride bikes, of course. The real point is that if you know what you're doing and avoid rash actions, you're less likely to get hurt.

SURVIVAL IN THE LAND
OF THE FOUR-WHEELED GAS GUZZLERS

Be aware. Be defensive. Be predictable. Be visible. Those are the keys to survival. If you should, in spite of the statistically low odds for intelligent adult riders, get wiped-out, be legally correct. Under the "no-fault" insurance laws pedestrians and cyclists still have the right to sue. You must be able to show that the driver was negligent and that you in no way did something to contribute to the cause of the accident. If you were not obeying the traffic laws or by your actions did something that contributed to the cause of the accident, you are considered equally guilty and will have difficulty collecting damages.

PROTECTIVE CLOTHING

The most basic and most ignored protective factor that you can control is the clothing you wear. It is well documented that light-colored cars—red, white, yellow and orange—are involved in significantly fewer accidents than are darker cars, blue, brown, or black. Blaze orange may seem a bit ostentatious, but black is more dignified on a casket than a bicycle. You have a choice—ridiculously visible or fashionably dead. Most bicycle fatalities are among the young, and what are the fashionable colors among that age group? Khaki, olive drab, blue denim, black—all good camouflage colors.

Beware that your blaze orange jacket doesn't lead to gross overconfidence. The driver who gets you will invariably plead, "I didn't see him until it was too late." In one encounter, the auto driver complained of cataracts. He managed to navigate by following the white line that marked the edge of the highway. There is also a population of the perpetually stoned, who account for about half of all highway fatalities.

In any legal action, one attempts to paint the other driver all black and one's self lily-white (or blaze orange). If either you or your surviving kin wear that blaze orange jacket during cross examination, it will have quite an impact on the jury.

Another important clothing factor is trouser cuffs. Roll them up, pin them down, tape them, use trouser bands, whatever, but make them secure. Don't rely on so-called chainguards. Things still have a way of getting caught. An enmeshed pants leg can throw you quite badly—fatally. If you are lucky you may only contact the cyclist's disease known as road rash. I once asked a road racer why he shaved his legs. Theoretically, at cycling speeds hairy legs should have lower air resistance than shaved legs. "Air resistance? I do it so it doesn't hurt when they rip the bandages off!" Meditate on that a bit.

WISDOM OF THE STREETS

There is order in traffic. This is because we have mutually agreed on a set of behaviors for drivers of vehicles. In defined situations we can make reasonable predictions as to the probable behavior of the other driver and act accordingly. And we have set down a list of penalties for those who do not follow the rules.

Though traffic laws allow you to predict the other driver's *probable* behavior, you must always consider the alternatives if your prediction is not correct. This is what is meant by being *aware* and *defensive*. You must constantly assess traffic as it evolves. You make reasonable predictions based on continuous assessments. That is being aware. Then you consider what will happen if your prediction fails.

You predict the parked car is empty. What if it pulls out? What if the door suddenly opens? The passing car turns in front of you. What then? That's being defensive. Better yet, be paranoid. Assume that anything that moves is deliberately plotting to jump into your path. Gravel and pot holes were put there by the city planner for your destruction. Dogs are rabid killers. Pedestrians are suicidal.

Traffic laws demand that the more powerful yield to the weak. Motor boats yield to boats under sail, cyclists yield to pedestrians, and cars yield to bicycles. Don't count on it—ever. In most states you are considered a vehicle and co-equal with the automobile on the roadway, but that's only in the eyes of the law. In competition, your 150 pounds and bicycle are no match for 4,000 pounds of automobile. Make your behavior predictable, even if the car driver's isn't.

There exists an unfortunate popular mythology of bicycle riding, one part of which states that cyclists should ride facing traffic on the left side of the roadway, as do pedestrians. This myth is perpetuated by the rather deep-rooted idea that the bicycle is a toy and not to be considered a serious means of transportation. The main argument is that you will see danger approaching and can take more effective evasive action. That may *sound* logical. In actual practice it is probably the biggest and most fatal error the beginner can make.

In the first place, riding on the left is illegal. If you are riding in violation of traffic laws at the time of an accident, you may find it impossible to recover damages. Riding against the flow of traffic may make it impossible for you to recover physically, too. If you ride on the left side of the road, no one will expect your presence and direction at driveways and intersections, so your accident probability increases astronomically. You might escape alive in the rare hit-from-behind situation; a head-on collision is ghastly. Rear-end and side-swiping collisions are the least frequent bicycle/car involvements. Rear-enders that do occur usually involve the cyclist initiating some behavior that was not predictable.

The pedestrian walks facing traffic because he has greater lateral mobility and can easily stop at corners. The pedestrian is given the edge in taking evasive action if danger is perceived. The argument that the same is true for the bicycle doesn't stand up in practice. To avoid that car coming at you all you have to do is swerve or jump off? Try that sometime—jump off indeed! If there is a line of parked cars on your left, just where are you to jump or swerve?

The toy bicycle mentality seems to be unaware that it doesn't take phenomenal ability to sustain an average speed of 15 mph for over 100 miles on a bicycle, and that for short distances, most anybody can approach 30 mph on level ground. On downhill runs, bikes often equal or exceed the speed of prevailing traffic. Consider the case of a car going 30 mph and a bicycle rolling in the same direction at 20 mph. The bicycle is being overtaken at only 10 mph. If the bicycle is on a curve and is not visible to the motorist until they are only 100 feet apart, the motorist still has almost seven seconds to perceive, make a decision and take evasive action.

Given the same speeds but a head-on approach, the car is gaining on the bicycle at 50 mph. With the same 100 feet of visibility the driver has a bit more than one second to perceive, decide and evade. Average tested perception and decision time is about 3/4-second. In the first instance you are hit at 10 mph. In the second you're hit at 50 mph. Still want to ride on the left side of the road?

The physical damage that occurs in a crash is related to the amount of energy that must be absorbed. This energy is absorbed in the work done deforming the vehicles and their occupants. The vehicle with the least mass will be deformed (how about "maimed") most. Energy is related to the *square* of the speed (the speed times itself). Compare 10 x 10 to 50 x 50. In the cases above, 25 times more energy must be absorbed in the head-on crash than in the rear-end approach.

For more on crashes, I recommend the following articles in *Bike World* magazine:

Surviving Car-Bike Crashes
William Sanders, October 1973, pp. 22-23.

Tuck 'n' Roll Trick
Jeff Foster, November 1974, pp. 16-17.

Another protective choice you have is to wear a helmet. Whether you consider them fashionable is hardly relevant. Like parachutes, also hardly fashionable, they are damned handy when you need one. Bicycling helmets have rather specialized requirements, one of the most important being ventilation. It can get rather hot and stuffy in a motorcyclist's helmet. Even a hockey helmet and the traditional cyclist's leather helmet can get quite warm. Contrary to what you may have learned in military service, your *head* is your most precious possession. Save that and the other end will take care of itself. At this writing, there were two excellent helmets for cycling on the market, the Bell and MSR models. Each has its shortcomings. The Bell's airscoops may be perilously close to the skull. The MSR is a trifle hot. Both of them whistle in the wind. The Skid-Lid II, a new design, has holes that expose your head to penetration damage (curbs, pedals, rocks, etc.). Its "breakaway" chin strap is not the safety factor its maker claims—you need protection on the second bounce! The older MSR has proved its worth in 18 severe crashes to the date of this writing, and either it or the Bell should be considered basic cycling gear.

The following *Bike World* articles by John Forester will greatly enhance your survival potential:

Emergency Maneuvers
December 1973

Dodging Traffic I & II
January 1974/February 1974

Changing Lanes in Traffic
April 1974

Review all your close calls in traffic relative to these articles and you will see how many of those situations were invited and could have been avoided.

Most laws governing bicycles imply something about riding as far to the right as possible or as far to the right as practical. I, and most long-time cyclists, prefer the latter choice of words. No vehicle operator has the right to obstruct traffic and let a long line of traffic pile up and not get by. Yet regardless of the words chosen, they mean "the right of the roadway," not the *shoulder* of the road. If the cars don't drive there, you don't either.

The inexperienced bicyclist tends to follow the "far to the right" rule slavishly. This can be dangerous. The shoulder of the roadway is a poor place to ride, the surface being usually very poor and not intended for traffic at all. Debris is swept onto the shoulder by passing traffic—it's a nice place to have open for an emergency dodge, but if you're already there, where else can you go?

The extreme right should be avoided under the following conditions:

● When it is obstructed with debris, pot holes, parked cars, people and storm drain gratings; do not swerve in and out to avoid those hazards, but stay far enough left that they can be avoided and so you can ride in a straight, *predictable* path.

● When passing another vehicle, *always* pass left unless the other vehicle is in the left lane. What if that double parked car opens its right hand door as you pass between it and the legally parked cars? Where do you go? Right—to the hospital.

● When approaching driveways and side streets, riding a straight line just off the edge of the right auto lane makes you more visible and provides a safety zone should a car start to back out of a drive or roll forward from a side street.

● Look far enough ahead so you don't have to swerve to avoid obstacles. Always look to see what the situation is behind you before moving left. This does two things: it informs you (be aware!); and your body language and eye contact gives the following traffic a hint as to your intention. Ease out slowly.

At times, when your speed is equal to or exceeds the flow of traffic, it is safest to move out and occupy the middle of your lane. You cannot afford to hit even small objects at higher speeds and you are less likely to get cut off at an intersection. As your speed decreases, move back to the right. If you are going fast enough to pass traffic in the right lane, move out into the legal passing lane. Do not attempt to pass by going between vehicles. Should either car swerve, you have no exit.

A constant complaint (and legitimate worry) of cyclists is the danger of car doors opening. You can lessen the danger a bit by not riding as far to the right on streets with parked cars. This position makes you visible for a greater distance. You can develop the comforting and invaluable habit of looking through the back window of every parked car for a driver who might be about to exit.

The few Archie Bunker types who'll insist that "you weirdo bike freaks stick to the sidewalks" and who'll attempt to hit you, throw objects at, or otherwise harass you can be arrested and successfully prosecuted. Make it a habit to get license numbers, color and type of vehicle, and description of the occupants. It may take a little of your time but it will make bicycle transportation a little safer for all. Personal experience tells me it's easier to get laws enforced against people than against dogs, leash laws being notoriously ineffective.

Know the phone number of your local state police unit. They are the most reliable and best-trained assistance you can obtain. Avoid police units filled by political appointees. Their training is often minimal and the person about whom you may be complaining may have political pull. Even if you are in the right and the officer is sympathetic, he may not be able to do much. State police generally know how to handle matters to avoid political hassles.

NEGOTIATING INTERSECTIONS

The majority of accidents occur at intersections. That

shouldn't be too surprising. With just a side street on your right, there are three ways to get clobbered. The car passing on your left turns right across your path—*splat!* The car approaching in the other lane cuts across your path—*zap!* The car waiting at the stop sign pulls out just as you get in front of it—*crunch!* If you ride hugging the curb, you invited the first case. If you are far enough left, far enough out to clear an actual or imaginary line of parked cars, it will not be possible to have that happen.

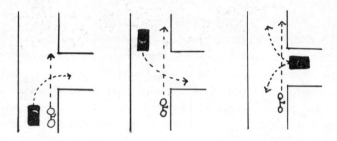

The latter two cases can be avoided. Establish eye contact. Do not indicate in any way that you are intimidated, but be prepared to get cut off. If you cannot get eye contact, no communication has taken place and the other driver may not even be aware of your presence. Not too many can look you directly in the eye and run you over. But don't count on that, either. If you look like you will back down, you'll be expected to. Watch the driver's actions; they often indicate intentions. The car that nervously edges forward is most likely to cut you off.

If there is traffic passing you at the time, it is unlikely you'll be cut off. However, if you are the only other vehicle present, expect anything. Get your fingers on the brakes. You are now prepared to either accelerate or brake as the situation demands.

The car at the side street waiting to turn left presents similar problems. Establishing eye contact can be a bit more difficult. The driver often looks to his right away from you until traffic in that direction is clear. Then the line of sight is quickly switched to the car's left. If it is clear—zoom! Meanwhile you have moved to some place in between two points of vision and are now right in front of the car—crunch!

Be particularly cautious if you are the only other vehicle on the scene. The best you can do is *look* like you have the right of way as before and be prepared to brake or haul it as the situation demands. Again, be alert to the other driver's body language. Remember always: drivers are looking out for cars, which are at least five feet wide. How wide are you?

Also, be alert to the following:

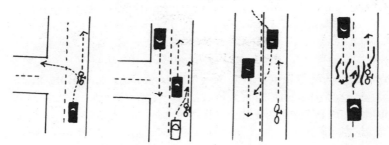

"Y" intersections are particularly difficult to negotiate. If your speed can approach that of the motor traffic, then move to the center of the lane. If this speed is not possible and the way is not clear, go to the spot marked x and wait. Cross on foot by the shortest route when it becomes safe to do so. Remount and continue along your route.

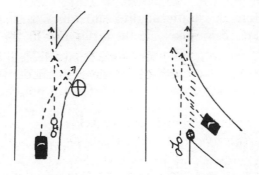

If you are a regular commuter, a little reconnaisance of alternative routes can greatly reduce the potential traffic hassles. You can often eliminate many hazardous intersections by selecting a route which eliminates places where you have to cross the traffic stream. The choice is yours.

A couple of tips on left turns. Since you're a vehicle with all the rights of other vehicles, you can turn left from the left-turn lane. If traffic speed and volume make it impossible for you to get over to the left-turn lane, ride on through the intersection and wait until the light changes for cross-traffic. When turning left from the left-turn lane, stay on the *right* side of the lane. Many bicyclists feel safer with a foot on the curb of the center island, but when the light goes green they find themselves trapped inside the flow of left-turning traffic, with no way to drift back over to the right. If you feel uneasy standing in the right side of the left turn lane, with traffic breezing past your shoulder at 35 mph, do the obvious: go to the head of the left-turn lane and move over in front of the first car in line. When the light turns green, check for late "intersection stormers," then ride straight ahead a bit, out of the way of left-turning cars.

TIPS FOR COMMUTERS

• Examine all possible routes. Select the route that has the fewest crossings of streets with heavy traffic flow. In two equal cases, take the one with the best surface, fewest dogs, children and other hazards.

• Explore this route at different times. Just five minutes earlier or later can make a great difference in traffic density.

• Once the route and time have been selected, try and ride at the same time every day. This way you encounter the same people and they will come to anticipate your presence.

• Know the number of the state police station with jurisdiction where you ride. Not only may it be useful to you but you may be able to help someone else. Car drivers have troubles too. Get involved if you are a witness. Someday you may need someone to do the same for you.

IN CASE OF AN ACCIDENT

In spite of all precautions, an accident may still occur. What

A successful San Diego, Calif. physician, Dr. Clifford Graves is one of the most eloquent spokesmen for around-town cycling.

can you do? Wear that protective helmet, and perhaps carry a small first aid kit.

Make a game of noting license numbers and descriptions of cars and motorists. An accident may leave you in an emotional state that will make it difficult to function. A little practice in observation will make you more reliable under conditions of stress. That may seem a bit paranoid, but it's paid off for me. Several times I have had a car pass me only to come upon that same car pulled over a few miles ahead. This would repeat several times. It turned out to be a neighbor clocking me just to see how fast I traveled by bike. Yet what if it had been someone looking for a good bike to rip off?

Carry some 3x5 cards and a pencil or pen that writes under a wide range of temperatures and wetness. Don't trust memory, write things down. In an emergency get the following information, in this order:

- license number
- color of vehicle
- type and model of vehicle
- description of driver and occupants
- name of the driver's insurance company (if the driver stays at the scene, or later if arrested)
- all details of the situation you can recall:
a. your location and direction of travel at the time
b. the location and direction of travel of other vehicles
c. diagram the above and show approximate distances
d. names and addresses of any witnesses (license numbers if they are unwilling)
e. list weather and light conditions at the time
f. the time of day and the date
- write down any remarks made by the other driver and/or witnesses

Do not make any statements about yourself except name, rank and serial number. Answer all questions of the investigating officer calmly and briefly. Do not make any accusations.

You might put respectful questions such as, "Do you think a breathalizer test might be in order?" "Is it possible to tell if the other driver was on drugs?" Otherwise most violations will be obvious. The professional police officer knows what questions to ask and when to ask them. Get the name of the investigating officer.

Usually insurance companies will be quite cooperative if it is evident that you were in the right. If you suffer severe injury and many medical expenses, it would be wise to consult with your attorney.

DOGS

Another hazard of the highway is man's so-called "best friend." Leash laws are mostly an unenforceable farce. Attack by one human being upon another leads to immediate arrest; dog owners get warnings.

Until you are bitten, the best you can hope for is to ward off the beast. Everything imaginable has been used: tire pumps, buggy whips, spray cans, air horns, pen guns that shoot blanks, starter's guns and even firearms. The latter are definitely *not* recommended. What if the owner shoots back? Does he know a blank from a live cartridge? Keep in mind that most dog owners are totally irrational when it comes to the welfare of their pets.

One weapon that proved very effective is the pistol-grip style sprayer. "Fantastik" cleaner comes with one and Amway sells a dandy for about 85 cents. Replace the quart-size bottle with a smaller flat hand lotion or shampoo bottle. Fit this with a loop of coat hanger wire and tape so that it hangs freely from your hip pocket. There is no fumbling to get it into position or to aim it. If it is always kept full, it requires little priming. Don't piddle around with what you put in it. Use the strongest ammonia you can get. After several years and multiple doses of 27-30% ammonia, I have yet to see a hound chasing after me with a white cane. I also lace mine with my own extract of home-grown Mexican red-hot peppers. The results have been most gratifying.

A Street Cyclist Testifies

BY JAMES CARSON

I am a college instructor; specifically I teach courses relating to ecology and the environment. In lecturing on certain conservation measures like air pollution control and gasoline rationing, I was often asked by my students if I practiced what I preached. Embarrassingly, I had to tell them I did not, at least not always. Realizing the credibility gap I was creating between my students and myself I decided to perform a conservation experiment which I have called the bicycle experiment.

During the past year I have not owned, driven, or *ridden* in an automobile. My requirements for local personal transportation have been met using only a bicycle. All my shopping trips have been done on a bike, as well as trips back and forth to work, to deliver the children to the nursery, to picnics and even to school.

During this time I have not made a single car payment, paid a single automobile insurance premium, bought any car tags or paid any license fees, bought a single gallon of gasoline, worried about getting a good deal from a car dealer, been frustrated by the gasoline shortage, received a single traffic or parking ticket, had to worry about finding a parking space, or struggled with heavy traffic. In addition, I calculate I have saved a minimum of $125 per month. In this time of high food prices I can appreciate this savings, particularly with two growing children.

More important than the monetary rewards, I contend, are the physical rewards. Since I have been biking continuously, I have enjoyed excellent physical health. I have more stamina to get through a day's lectures and research and still have energy to enjoy my children and work in my garden in the evening. My reflexes are better than they have ever been, my lung capacity has increased, and I have a certain zest for living which I had never experienced before I started biking.

The nice part of all this is that none of this physical well being had to come about from strenuous exercise, only bicycling, which at all times was quite pleasurable.

A dividend of the good health I enjoy is that now I feel more relaxed and unhurried. I am able to pace myself every day and I have a keener awareness of what I am capable of accomplishing. I have also developed more patience and learned to plan ahead. Several of my colleagues have taken up biking at my suggestion and report similar feelings.

In slowing down (temperamentally and in traffic) I have been able to savor the nice things about the outdoors that were lost to me when I was inside an automobile. Riding to work on a bike I can literally touch and taste the dew on the leaves and relish the song of the cardinal. I can breathe deeply the crisp clean morning air and almost feel the oxygen being taken up in my bloodstream and transported to all the tissues of my body as I use my own muscle power to propel myself in my chosen direction. I can see, feel, and smell many of the natural wonders that I speak of in the classroom. As a result I can appreciate them more and I am able to help my students to appreciate them more. I can get none of these sensations in an automobile.

Many people say they simply cannot get along without a car. I believe this is a myth. I have gotten along just fine without one for over a year. There are occasions, I concur, when an automobile does have an advantage over a bicycle, such as in time of medical emergency, or for business reasons.

Someone once calculated just how much money the average person spends on automobiles from the time a driver's license is first obtained until death, along with the interest that money would have earned if it were invested elsewhere. The total comes to about $200,000. This was figured using an economy car and when gasoline was 32 cents per gallon, and assumed no serious accidents would occur.

Environmentally and aesthetically, the bike is head and shoulders above the automobile. With a bike there is no gasoline shortage, no hydrocarbon and lead pollution, no necessity for vast networks of highways, no noises, nothing like the auto's

70,000 deaths per year, and I have never seen a bicycle junkyard blighting the landscape.

For those who fear to face the elements on a bicycle, I have found that carefully chosen clothing and proper planning will sustain the cyclist quite nicely in sub-zero weather. In fact, I ride my bike to work rather comfortably in weather where automobiles have been forced off the road because of ice and snow—provided they could be started in the first place.

On a more personal level, I have begun to think of fashion without purpose as a philosophy open to ridicule.

It is also important to the cyclist who rides in all kinds of weather to eat properly. I find many of the highly processed foods being sold in the store today are losing their market among cyclists. As a result I hope that new markets will be recognized for foods conducive to good health.

I find it both humorous and sad at the same time when I meet people struggling at eight-to-five jobs they despise in order to make car payments so they will have a way to get to work. They have never enjoyed life as much as I have this past year while conducting my bicycle experiment.

Chapter 2

Getting Ready To Roll

Buying a bicycle is a specialist's art. It takes special knowledge. Walk into a bike shop and you're at the salesman's mercy unless you know the terms of the trade. Walk in when the mechanics are engaged in one of the traditional, endless debates over comparative component quality, and you won't understand a word.

Brand-name buying is a fairly reliable way to steer clear of trouble when buying a new bicycle. But if you're in the used bicycle market, remember the hidden defects of used cars. Bent frames, scored bearing races, micro-fractured metal parts, components with underground reputations for poor durability and precision—these are just a few of the perils of used-bike-buying.

A bicycle's quality is the sum of the quality of its parts. If your frame has Reynolds double-butted 531 tubes throughout and your derailleur is the Campagnolo Gran Turismo, you've got—possibly—a good frame, but you've definitely got a mediocre derailleur. We obviously don't have space here to review in detail all the components ever made, so we'll talk about general principles that will help you spot quality.

When in doubt, whom do you ask—without getting buried

in a lot of magazine research? First off, a warning. Faddism is rampant in cycling. A large group of "serious cyclists" have plenty of ego energy tied up in specific components. If they tell you Reynolds 531 tubing isn't as good as Columbus, find out if they've just invested hundreds of dollars in a Columbus-tubed bicycle. They'll tell you Campagnolo sidepull brakes—at over $100 the set—are the only ones worth buying—of course, omitting to mention that 90 of 110 bikes ridden in the first stage of the 1959 Tour de France, the greatest race in the world, had Mafac Racer centerpull brakes, which cost less than one-fourth as much as Campy sidepulls.

The needs of the around-town cyclist and those of the racer are vastly different. Later on we'll give suggestions for improving your bike's efficiency without mortgaging your home. Meanwhile, keep in mind that dedicated cyclists of many years' racing, touring and commuting experience often ride humble gear. Tom Cuthbertson, author of the great *Anybody's Bike Book*, cruises around Santa Cruz, Calif., on a three-speed. He even takes it on training rides with racing cyclists. (Tom's in pretty good shape!) The three-speed has been ridden comfortably on 30-day crossings of the continental United States. It's the standby of many an old-time English cycle tourist, who'll sneer at the mention of 10 speeds. The editor of *Bike World* magazine hotdogs around on a good but less-than-one-up Motobecane Mirage while his racing bike with its delicate sewup tires sits at home awaiting the weekend hard ride. He feels he gets more training effect per mile on his 35-pound "truck."

THINGS TO LOOK FOR WHEN BUYING A BIKE

Bike quality ranges from self-destructing trash to hand-built professional machines costing $1000+. You can put together yourself, or buy assembled, a very durable used 10-speed bicycle for under $100 (early-1975 prices), if you're lucky and know your components. Normally, you should expect to pay at least $100 for a decent, reconditioned bike of the Peugeot UO-8/Raleigh Grand Prix/Motobecane Mirage class. *Any* bike, new or used, can disappoint you with little replacements and service jobs that add up in cost. In this chapter we'll run through some things you'd better know before falling in love with a nice-looking bicycle. Keep in mind, also, that a Reynolds 531 frame is dandy, but a bent one is not; that a Campy Nuovo Record derailleur is the ultimate, but if it's been crash-damaged, it may be worthless.

To come back to our earlier question: whom do you turn to when you need simple answers quickly? Don't overlook the bike shop mechanic. You should be able to tell the "faddy" from the person of experience and reason just by comparing opinions, voice volumes, etc.   How do you know the guy who touts Sun Tour derailleurs isn't singing their virtues because he's overstocked? Again, shop around, get to know people, weigh your experience in the calm atmosphere of your own home, away from all that glittering, highly tempting componentry. A fairly good standard of quality prevails in the competitive $100-$200 class, with somewhat more caution needed in the $100-$140 range, where cost-cutting via cheap derailleurs, brakes, saddles, etc., is rampant. Some of the "consumer" bike-buying books are so bad as to be worthless—avoid them.

Here, then, are the basic principles for judging bicycle quality.

• **Lugged frame construction.** Lugs are fancy sockets into which frame tubes are inserted for greater strength. If one tube simply butts up to another in a welded joint, the necessary strength must be supplied by heavier-walled tubing, making the bike very heavy. Beware of "pasted on" material made to look like lugs. There are very high-quality unlugged bicycles made by custom builders and selling at very high prices. Some cheaper unlugged bikes are also quite durable—the Schwinns, for instance—but most are quite heavy for long-distance use.

• **Tubular fork construction.** Avoid a solid fork. The solid fork is heavier, absorbs road shock poorly, and has less lateral strength than tubular construction.

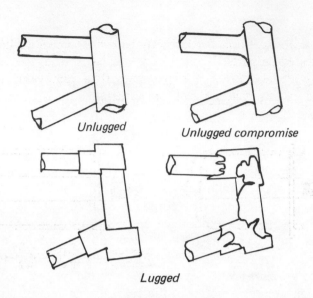

Unlugged   *Unlugged compromise*

Lugged

● **Fork ends (Drop outs).** Avoid stamped-out or spot-welded construction.

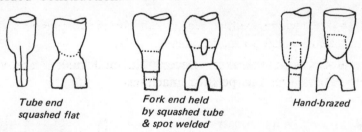

Tube end squashed flat   *Fork end held by squashed tube & spot welded*   *Hand-brazed*

● **Axle assembly.** The axle assembly should have a distinct cone, lock washer, and lock nut. Look for a groove or keyway at the axle end as evidence.

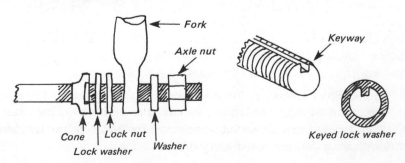

Fork

Axle nut

Keyway

Cone   *Lock nut*

Lock washer   *Washer*

Keyed lock washer

● **Hubs.** Look for hubs that do not appear to have seams or pressed-on parts.

● **Pedals.** Look for pedals with a removable dust cap. Avoid pedals that cannot be adjusted.

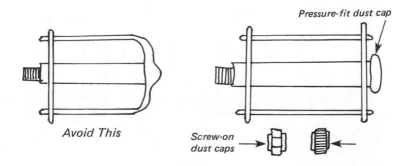

Avoid This

Pressure-fit dust cap

Screw-on dust caps →

● **Three-piece cranks.** Avoid the "Ashtabula" one-piece type.

● **Wire-frame saddle.** Watch out for cheap plastic saddle frames and stapled-on saddle covers.

● **Center-pull brakes.** Decent side-pull brakes are very rarely found on inexpensive machines.

Center-pull brakes   *Side-pull brakes*

● **Shift levers on the down tube.** Other locations use more cable and housing and more bends, thus more friction. Stem-mounted levers can be hazardous to the groin in an accident. You also pay more for this style.

● **Tires.** Wired-on "clincher" tires that inflate to 65 lbs or more.

● **Weight.** Total weight should be about 27-33 lbs for comfortable riding at 5-100 miles.

● **Accessories:**
a. toe clips and straps
b. tire pump
c. light plastic fenders (if you're an all-weather rider)
d. head and tail lights as well as reflectors

● **Avoid these accessories.** These are sold with the inexperienced klotz in mind:
a. brake extenders or so called "safety" levers
b. kick stands
c. chain guards (wear trouser clips)
d. spoke protectors (keep your derailleur properly adjusted!)
e. derailleur guards

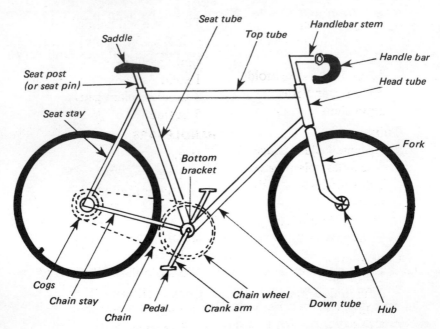

VALUE CHECK LIST

The following checklist can be used as a guide to the comparative value of bicycles. The higher the sum for the components, the more valuable the bicycle. Unless the difference is more than five points, it should not be considered significant. Examine the machine component by component and sum up the values. The range is from 24 to 157. At one time this number even approximated the retail price. Today multiply by two to get approximate price. Tomorrow the proportionality constant will be closer to three. Note: points here are given for cash value—*not* in all cases by desirability. Tubular tires, for example, are more expensive but not always more desirable. In other cases, such as the recessed-bolt handlebar stem, paying more gives you a safety "extra" or, in the case of expensive frame tubes, an advantage in lightness and responsiveness. For some background on the selection of points, see the section on increasing the efficiency of a bicycle.

FRAME

    1 high carbon
    5 chrome/molybdenum
    alloy
    10 Columbus, Reynolds
    531, Super Vitus or
    equivalent
Tubing
    1 seamed plain gauge
    3 seamless plain gauge
    5 double-butted main
    tubes
    10 double-butted
    throughout
Construction
    1 unlugged
    3 filleted welds,
    unlugged
    7 fully-lugged

FORK

    Type of Steel (same
    points as for frame)
    Construction
    1 solid
    3 tubular, plain gauge
    5 butted

HANDLEBARS

    Metal
        1 steel
        3 aluminum alloy

STEM

    Metal
        1 steel
        3 aluminum alloy
    Construction
        1 exposed bolt
        3 recessed bolt

CHAIN
> 1 1/2 x 1/8
> 3 1/2 x 3/32

SPOKES
> 1 plain gauge
> 3 double-butted

TIRES
Pressure Rating
> 1 55 lbs or less
> 3 65 lbs
> 5 75 lbs and up

Size
> 1 less than 26 inches
> 3 26 inches
> 5 27 inches

Type
> 1 clinchers
> 2 tubulars

RIMS
Metal
> 1 steel
> 3 aluminum alloy

Type
> 1 clinchers
> 3 tubulars

HUBS
Construction
> 1 several parts, seams evident
> 5 seamless

Metal
> 1 steel
> 3 aluminum alloy

Axles
> 1 cone and lock nut fused
> 5 cone, lock washer and lock nut separate parts

Attachment
> 1 standard nuts
> 3 wing nuts
> 5 quick release

CRANKS
> 1 one-piece (Ashtabula)
> 3 three-piece, cottered
> 5 three-piece, cotterless

CHAINWHEELS
> 1 steel
> 3 aluminum alloy

HEADSET
> 1 unmarked brand
> 3 brand name (Stronglight, Campagnolo, etc.)

PEDALS
Construction
> 1 one-piece cage, non-adjustable
> 5 adjustable cones

Metal
> 1 steel cage
> 3 aluminum alloy cage

FREEWHEEL
> 1 wide-ratio

3 close-ratio

SADDLE

1 padded with springs
3 no springs, padded
5 wire frame, leather
or plastic

DERAILLEUR

1 single piece of metal,
linkage easily bent
5 double pieces par-
allel-linked for extra
strength
7 double pieces in
aluminum alloy instead
of steel

BRAKES

Hand Lever
1 distance A divided
by distance B less
than 5.00
3 distance A divided
by distance B greater
than 5.00

Brake Arm
1 C less than D
2 C equals D
3 C greater than D
Metal
1 steel
3 aluminum alloy

ACCESSORIES

1 each for water bot-
tle, tool bag, reflectors
2 tools
3 tire pump
5 toe clips and straps

NEGATIVE FEATURES
Subtract points as follows:

1 less than 10 speed
2 banana seat
3 standard handlebars
4 high-rise handlebars
5 kick stand
7 brake extenders or
"safety" levers

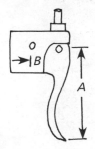
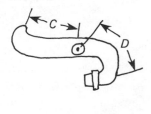

The numbers definitely are biased toward a machine with
specific features. This may be offensive to the person who loves

Makes you want to wheel one out for a ride, doesn't it? But be sure your new bike's custom-fitted. (OMPhoto)

their three-speed bicycle with standard all-rounder bars. It's a beautiful thing we have between ourselves and our bicycles, and let no person interfere.

FRAME SIZE AND SADDLE HEIGHT

Measure your inseam, crotch to floor, standing in stockinged feet. Subtract 9-10" from this inseam measurement to get your approximate frame size. The frame size is the distance from the center of the crank axle to the top of the seat tube. In actual practice you should be able to straddle the top tube while wearing the shoes in which you intend to ride. You then should be able to raise the front wheel ½-1" off the ground.

Get the proper frame size even for a child. The common practice is to buy a larger frame so the child will grow into it. If the frame is too large, the bicycle is difficult to control—it's possible that the child might not live long enough to grow into it.

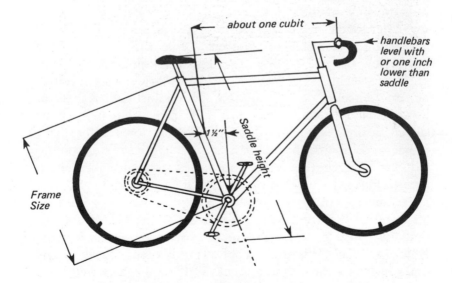

about one cubit

handlebars level with or one inch lower than saddle

1 ½"

Saddle height

Frame Size

Many of the inexpensive hand brakes cannot be operated effectively by children. Poor brakes combined with an overly large frame can be extremely dangerous.

Saddle height can be determined by multiplying the in-seam measurement found above by 1.09. (Studies of profes-sional cyclists have found this height most efficient for the majority of riders.) The height of the saddle is measured from the center of the pedal axle when the pedal is at its lowest position, with the crank arm in a direct line with the seat tube. Saddle height is measured from pedal axle to the top of the saddle. Loosen the saddle binder bolt (on the frame, not the saddle itself), set the saddle at the proper height, and re-tighten the binder bolt. The seat post should be tight enough that it takes a good chop to displace it sideways. There should be a good 2" of seat post down inside the seat tube. Get a longer seat post if necessary.

The top of the saddle can be horizontal, front tip just slightly higher than the rear (preferred by most male riders), or slightly down-tilted (preferred by many women).

The front tip of the saddle should be about 1½" behind the center line of the crank axle.

After saddle height and position have been set, the handle-bars should be adjusted for comfort. A rule of thumb is an inch or so below the top of the saddle, but this is an individual mat-ter. Racers set their bars so 45% of bike-and-rider weight is over the front wheel, 55% over the rear. This adjustment is made at the stem binder bolt. Loosen the bolt until it has risen about half an inch, then tap the head of the bolt down with a light hammer. Position the handle bars and re-tighten the stem binder bolt. With the wheel between your knees, it should take a sharp force to move the bars sideways. You do want a little "give" in case of an accident.

The tilt of the dropped position is set at the binder bolt to-ward the rear axle until you decide you're more comfortable some other way. This angle is set at the binder bolt where the handlebars pass through the stem. Tighten the bars well—you don't want them to swing up suddenly when you're pulling hard on a steep hill.

The brake levers should be set according to your own finger reach and strength. If the lever is too close, you can pull it right to the bar without 100% braking power. If the lever is set too high, you might not be able to give it an optimal squeeze.

If you have standard handlebars, you can approximate the effect of dropped bars by turning them upside down. Have the ends of the handlebars stopped with a big, fat plug, sold in bike shops, to prevent severe injury in a fall.

The distance from saddle tip to handlebar should be about the same as from the tip of your middle finger to your elbow.

(Inseam measurement—all dimensions in inches)

Inseam	Frame Size	Saddle Height
25	15	27.25
25.5	16	27.795
26	16	28.340
26.5	17	28.8850
27	17	29.43
27.5	18	29.9750
28	18	30.52
28.5	19	31.065
29	19	31.610
29.5	20	32.1550
30.5	20	
30.5	21	33.2450
31	21	33.790
31.5	22	34.335
32	22	34.88
32.5	23	35.4250
33	23	35.970
33.5	24	36.5150
34	24	37.060
34.5	25	37.605
35	25	38.15
35.5	26	38.6950
36	26	39.240
37.5	27	39.785
37	27	40.330

GEAR RATIOS

The little gears on the back wheel which in the past may have been referred to as sprockets, are more generally called cogs. On multi-geared bicycles with derailleur shift mechanisms, the cogs are clustered on a device called the freewheel. On track bicycles, the cog attaches directly to the hub and coasting (freewheeling) is not possible. This is known as a fixed gear. The sprockets up front where the pedals are, are referred to as chainwheels.

Bike shops can do most gear changes in minutes.   (OMPhoto)

Experienced cyclists do not refer to first gear, third gear or 10th gear as motorists do. More information is communicated by stating the number of cog teeth and the number of chainwheel teeth being used. The cyclist will say, "I was pushing a 52/14." Another way of expressing gears is to state the gear number in inches. This number is the ratio of chain wheel teeth to cog teeth times the wheel diameter in inches. Thus, a 100-inch gear for a 27-inch wheel is a 52-tooth chainwheel and a 14-tooth cog:

$$\frac{52 \times 27}{14} = 100.3$$

A bicycle with a 20-inch wheel, 65-tooth chainwheel, and a 13-tooth cog would also have a 100-inch gear. Both cyclists would travel the same distance for one complete revolution of the cranks.

Gear numbers in inches refer back to the diameter of the front wheel of one of the old-fashioned highwheelers that would take you the same distance for one complete revolution of the cranks as a modern cog/chainwheel combination.

A 100-inch gear =

100 inches

A now surpassed bicycle speed record was established behind a wind screen attached to a racing car at 129 miles per hour. This bicycle had a 278-inch gear. An equivalent penny-farthing bike would have a wheel 23 feet in diameter. Imagine taking a header from up there at 129 miles an hour!

Pedaling along at the conservative cadence of 60 rpm in a 278-inch gear will carry you at a neat 49-50 miles per hour—in theory. In actual practice, air resistance soon takes the zip out of your efforts. You will find that you have a Rolls Knardly instead of a Rolls Royce. (Rolls like mad down the hills but knardly make it up the other side.)

The true purpose of gearing is not to get you up the hills more easily or down them faster, but to enable you to maintain a constant pedaling cadence over varied terrain and wind conditions. Just as a distance runner attempts to maintain a constant stride, a constant pedaling cadence makes the most efficient use of human energy expenditure.

GEAR RATIOS FOR 27-INCH DIAMETER WHEELS

Cog Teeth	Chain Wheel Teeth										
	34	36	38	40	42	44	46	48	50	52	54
12	77	81	86	90	95	99	104	108	112	117	122
13	71	75	79	83	87	91	96	100	104	108	112
14	66	69	73	77	81	85	89	93	96	100	104
15	61	65	68	72	76	79	83	86	90	94	97
16	57	61	64	68	71	74	78	81	84	88	91
17	54	57	60	64	67	70	73	76	79	83	86
18	51	54	57	60	63	66	69	72	75	78	81
19	48	51	54	57	60	63	65	68	71	74	77
20	46	49	51	54	57	59	62	65	68	70	73
21	44	46	49	51	54	57	59	62	64	67	69
22	42	44	47	49	52	54	56	59	61	64	66
23	40	42	45	47	49	52	54	56	59	61	63
24	38	41	43	45	47	50	52	54	56	59	61
25	37	39	41	43	45	48	50	52	54	56	58
26	35	37	39	42	44	46	48	50	52	54	56
27	34	36	38	40	42	44	46	48	50	52	54
28	33	35	37	39	41	42	44	46	48	50	52
29	32	34	35	37	39	41	43	45	47	48	50
30	31	32	34	36	38	40	41	43	45	47	49

SPEED IN MPH FOR 60 CRANK RPM WITH 27-INCH WHEELS

Cog Teeth	Chain Wheel Teeth										
	34	36	38	40	42	44	46	48	50	52	54
12	14	14	15	16	17	18	18	19	20	21	22
13	13	13	14	15	16	16	17	18	19	19	20
14	12	12	13	14	14	15	16	17	17	18	19
15	11	12	12	13	13	14	15	15	16	17	17
16	10	11	11	12	13	13	14	14	15	16	16
17	10	10	11	11	12	12	13	14	14	15	15
18	9	10	10	11	11	12	12	13	13	14	14
19	9	9	10	10	11	11	12	12	13	13	14
20	8	9	9	10	10	11	11	12	12	13	13
21	8	8	9	9	10	10	11	11	11	12	12
22	7	8	8	9	9	10	10	11	11	11	12
23	7	8	8	8	9	9	10	10	10	11	11
24	7	7	8	8	8	9	9	10	10	10	11
25	7	7	7	8	8	8	9	9	10	10	10
26	6	7	7	7	8	8	9	9	9	10	10
27	6	6	7	7	7	8	8	9	9	9	10
28	6	6	7	7	7	8	8	8	9	9	9
29	6	6	6	7	7	7	8	8	8	9	9
30	5	6	6	6	7	7	7	8	8	8	9

Chapter 3

Lightening The Load

Consider what makes the bicycle go and what opposes its going. Excluding hills, you have to push on the pedals, as any idiot knows. Common sense also shows that the harder you push, the faster you go under the same conditions. Unfortunately, the harder you 'push, the sooner you tire of the task. On a standard or touring-style bicycle, much of that energy is wasted.

Let's look at the things that retard your forward motion: gravity (on hills), mass (retards acceleration), internal friction, road surface friction, and air resistance. The greatest of these is air resistance. Those who've done much bike traveling prefer the grind through the Rockies to the headwinds of Kansas or the plains of Northern Europe. Any place with windmills is a place of heartbreak.

The prosaic (inevitable?) way to overcome resistance is to bull your way through. The energy supply is there—bean power—but the idea is to cut down on sneaky losses through mechanical inefficiencies. With a low stool, bathroom scales and some books you can do a few experiments that will show you how to cheat the devils of friction, inertia and wind. Put the scales on the floor in front of the stool. Sit on the stool with your back straight as if you were riding a bike with upright handlebars. Push on the scale as hard as you can. On a stool about 18 inches high, an average person weighing 130 pounds can exert about 36 pounds of pressure on the scale.

Now stack some books and magazines on the stool to raise your seat about six inches. With your back straight as before, try the force test again. In tests I've conducted, the force went up to 46 pounds. That is an increase of about 20%. Now go to the section on saddle height and see if yours is set properly. The cost so far? $0.00.

Repeat the force test, only this time lean forward as you press down. We now get 58 pounds. Check to see that your handlebars are set correctly in relation to the saddle. Perhaps they could be lowered. Standard handlebars can also be made into modified drops by turning them upside down and angling the hand grips forward. This again will cost nothing. If you shop around, these can be found for $2 or $3.

Dropped bars have advantages other than racy looks:

● They increase the force you can exert on the pedals.

● They take some of the load off your rear end and spine and distribute it to your arms.

● They decrease the area of your body that must push through the air.

To simulate the total effect of dropped bars, move your stool and scale near a heavy chair or sofa. Now, as you lean forward and press down with your foot, pull upward on the chair leg at the same time. One cyclist I know got 92 pounds. Compare that with the original 36 pounds. The dropped bars give you an advantage somewhat like rowing a boat. As you push with your feet, you pull with your arms. You are bringing muscles into the act that were just getting a free ride before.

A word of caution: dropped handlebars not only reduce your cross section to the wind, but they reduce your cross sectional visibility to other drivers. It'll also be harder to turn your head and look at the traffic behind you. As your efficiency and average speed increase, you will have to modify your traffic behavior accordingly. Up to this point it probably was rare for you to be moving at the speed of motor traffic. Now you may occasionally equal or exceed it in the city.

There is a good chance, even with everything properly adjusted and converted to dropped handlebars, that you are not using your feet to best advantage. Do you push with the ball of your foot? Do you know what "ankling" means? Proper ankling will increase the duration of your thrust on the pedals by increasing the arc through which you push. With proper ankling you can almost double the distance through which force is applied. Your energy output then will be about tripled. Basically, ankling is pushing forward with the heel lowered at the top of the pedal stroke and following through to the rear with your toe at the bottom of the stroke (heel raised). It starts to come naturally after you've been cycling awhile.

Up to this point the other foot has been getting a free ride on the upstroke. Think how much more efficient you would be if you could pull up with that foot. In our stool/bathroom scale demonstration, with a board under a chair rung as a lever, we found the rider could exert a 70-pound upward pulling force. This, combined with the previous 92 pounds, is a total of 162 pounds. Compare that with the original 36 pounds. Also keep in mind that our demonstrator weighed only 130 pounds. He exerted greater than his own weight in maximum force per pedal revolution without getting off the saddle. Now get off the saddle and add your own weight to the pedals and you can picture the tremendous work done by a racer in a hard "jump."

A decent set of rat trap pedals, toe clips and straps will run you a bit of cash, but they're worth it. Toe clips and straps almost force correct ankling. Avoid self-destructing throwaway pedals. Get a good set that can be maintained and adjusted. You should be able to do all of this for under $20. You can go all-out and buy racing pedals that might cost more than the original bicycle. But why do that?

Another nice energy-saver, but not essential for the commute rider, is alloy rims. They make a very real difference in the energy you have to put out. A well-known maxim among racing cyclists, who're deeply concerned with cycling efficiency, is,

"It's more important to take weight off the rims than the frame." That's because resistance to changes in speed is much greater out at the rim than it is at the hub or in the frame of the bike. Once you get up to cruising speed, there's little difference in effort between turning alloy and steel rims, but where frequent speed changes occur—a common situation for the commuter—light alloy rims can make a big difference. Ask your local bike shop to let you ride similar bikes with each type, and you'll see for yourself. If you want to keep your cycling budget down, scrounge around for old alloy wheels. We've found perfectly rideable ones for as low as $6.

The second highest resistance you have to overcome is the friction of your tires on the roadway. Proper tire inflation will reduce this. If your tires are only inflatable to 50 pounds, you might consider moving up to a higher-quality 90-pound tire. If you are particularly heavy and/or pack heavy loads on your machine while touring, a better set is almost vital. You can reduce the tread width as well, by going to 27 x 1 1/8" tires, which are used on standard 27 x 1 1/4" rims.

You can eliminate the useless "conveniences" that get tacked onto many bicycles. If you are a fairweather rider, take off the fenders. If you are an all-weather rider, you can get lightweight plastic fenders. The so-called mini-fenders are a useless bit of cosmetics. Full fenders are useful—they keep a considerable amount of crud out of the machinery, they keep you cleaner and drier front and rear, and if you wear glasses they can even be a safety factor in terms of increased visibility. If you cycle where livestock is part of the traffic, they are an aesthetic essential. There is crud and then there is crud.

Chain guards, spoke protectors and derailleur guards are designed for the klotz or the lazy. Use rubber bands, tape, clips, or just plain wrap your pant legs in your socks. Keep the rear derailleur properly adjusted and it won't go through the spokes. Lock your bike to something and it will not fall over.

The so-called "safety" levers or "brake extenders" have never been proved to be safe. They certainly do not stop as effectively as handgrip levers. In my own biased opinion they are at best a gimmick that may lead the rider into a false sense of security. The experienced rider looks ahead to anticipate the need to brake and has his or her fingers ready for emergencies. In a real emergency you may need all the braking power your system can deliver. "Safety" levers just cannot deliver. They have been known to snap off at just the wrong time. If you already have them, take them off. If you are buying a new bicycle that has them, have the store remove them as well as their extra cost from the price you pay. If the store is not willing to do both (you should save at least $3), go elsewhere.

The kickstand is probably the most useless piece of inconvenient convenience that has ever been attached to a bicycle. Ask yourself, did you ever really *need* that thing? The kickstand has probably led to more stolen bicycles than any other item since it's so easy to leave the bike standing unlocked. The weight of that kickstand would be better replaced by the weight of a lock and chain.

Consider the effort needed to lift 200 pounds six inches off the floor. Unless you're a dedicated "iron pusher," it's not something you'd ordinarily want to do. But every time you climb a vertical distance of 100 feet with that one-pound kickstand, you've done the same amount of work.

The next time you go shopping, total up the cost of chain guard, spoke protector, kickstand, "safety" levers and any other nonessentials. See if you can swing a deal to have them removed and others added for the same total price: toe clips and straps, a tire pump, a tire pressure gauge.

The greatest load of useless weight on your bicycle is suspended from your own frame. (See "Diet Versus Drilling," by Creig Hoyt, M.D., *Bike World*, June 1974, and "The Trouble With Being Fat," Creig Hoyt, M.D., *Bike World*, Sept. '74.) Unless you ride regularly a good distance at a good pace, it will be easier to deprive your mouth of a few pounds than to take them off your bicycle. The greatest benefit you can gain from cycling is increased cardiovascular efficiency. That does not come by lugging excess weight slowly up long hills in a super low gear, but from the oxygen uptake of a rapid pedalling cadence. Get out there and breathe a little. Minimal cardiovascular condition is achieved when you are able to ride at a heart rate of 130-150 for at least 15 minutes *continuously*, and for a total of one hour a week, with no more than three days off in a row. And you can forget about losing weight by cycling. It takes about 100 miles of riding to burn off a pound of fat. Not that cycling is ridiculously easy—fat is a ridiculously concentrated source of energy!

WHAT TO WEAR?

Wear what's safest for cycling and keep a change of clothes (including underwear) at work. Anything that can be damaged by rain is carried in plastic bags—your watch and wallet, for example. For cold weather, wear layers of clothing. It may be 20 below in the morning but 20 above when you come home.

Common sense told this girl the way to dress for a light drizzle and moderate cold on a Montana 100-mile ride. (Dan Burden)

If you have metal-framed glasses, protect the bridge of your nose in very cold weather. Frostbite is a real problem. Wear a full-face balaclava. Check the weather reports for the wind chill factor and dress according to *your* speed through the wind. If you average 10 mph through a 20-mph headwind, use 30 mph in selecting your wind-chill-equivalent clothing. Actually you will feel colder just standing around at 20 below than riding because of the heat your body generates while cycling. But you do have to protect yourself until that heat gets generated, which may take a few miles. Avoid clothing that does not breathe. Rubberized cloth and plastic keep the rain out but the perspiration in. You will drown in your own sweat, so you might as well just tolerate a bit of wetness.

It is an old wives' tale that wetness causes colds. Colds are the body's reaction to a stress crisis. Cold weather puts unaccustomed demands on the body's stress adaptation mechanisms. In most of us, poor dietary habits have created such a toxic load on the overworked organs of elimination that cold weather exposure is just adding insult to injury. In order to make itself ready for resisting cold weather, the body then bypasses ordinary channels of self-cleaning and massively eliminates accumulated poisons by way of the mucus membranes, etc. All the mucus that runs out from your nose and throat is loaded with accumulated (mostly dietary) poisons. That's why it tastes like salt—one of the most overconsumed food toxins in this country.

Disease is not an "attack" by germs, as medicine has long suspected. Hygienists have discovered that it's a process of *recovery* from a weakened condition. "Bad germs" just take the opportunity of temporarily-weakened resistance to "make hay while the sun shines"—they are an accompanying phenomenon of disease, not the cause. Hygienic living with proper diet, exercise and emotional life is the greatest disease preventive.

What's all this mean for the commuter in winter? If you're truly, hygienically clean inside and in strong condition, you'll have little to fear from riding "soaked" in a warm rain. If you face cold rain day after day, better look to more elaborate protection of the body's heat—even if you decide it's ok to get wet and change on arrival.

Clothing that will not breathe can be dangerous in freezing weather. The condensed perspiration freezes, the insulation value of the clothing is lost, and soon your flesh also freezes.

If you don't want to ride at night, intending to rely on reflectors, make a sunrise/sunset chart from the data for your area in the farmer's almanac. As long as it is not overcast, you can usually get by from about a half hour before sunrise with only a leg or armband light. Most other drivers have their head-lights on in the morning and your rear reflector will be doing its job. In the evening, however, reflectors will not be much good as too many drivers do not turn on their lights until after it has become too dark to see you well. You really need lights, front and rear, for night riding. Side reflectors are worthless as are reflectorized tires; a far-off driver will see you anyway in the path of his headlights. And side reflectors don't come into play any sooner in a sudden-approach crash (driveway, alley, side street) than does normal headlight sighting.

If you use rechargeable batteries, get two sets for each light. Have one set charging during the day and ride with the other. Switch over to the fresh set when you return at night. Some of the tail lights that use one D cell can be improved by making your own battery from four AA cells. Two cells are con-nected in series and these are then connected in parallel. This will double the voltage and quadruple the brightness. (It will also halve the bulb life, so carry extras.)

GOING LONGER

For long trips, say 100 miles or more, the following things must be considered:

- water
- sunburn
- food
- physical condition
- tools and spares

Your biggest problems will probably be water and sun-burn. If you pace yourself and take it slow and easy, you and just about anyone else can travel for about 10 or 12 hours with only a few short rest stops. However, most people aren't prepared to be out in the sun that long. A sunburn of only a few hours can have very serious consequences—it's no laughing matter and can even be fatal. Gradual conditioning to the sun should be part of your overall physical conditioning. Light protective clothing is also advised. Full-length sleeves and trousers may seem ridiculous when it is 90° in the shade, but may save you greater discomfort and a trip to the hospital. The cooling effect of cycling can hide the warning signs of sunburn.

The Arizona desert begins and the Sierras fade away as Phil Garner catches a drink during his cross-US trip by 3-speed.

Water is not as easy to get as one might think. It is very easy to get yourself into some really remote places on a bicycle that would not be a problem at all in a car. Thirty miles to the nearest water by bicycle could be more of an ordeal than you bargained for.

Drink before you feel thirsty and eat before you feel

hungry. Sip and munch. Know where you will find your next water supply. If you find an earlier source, fill up then. Do not run out. The weight of an extra water bottle is better than the weight of a solid gold kickstand.

Avoid fatty foods and protein, which take the most energy to digest. The "high protein for athletes" myth has been debunked in hundreds of laboratory experiments. The body requires only tiny extra amounts of protein, if any at all, for even severe endurance exercise. Avoid white sugar; not only is it suspected of causing certain types of cancer and arteriosclerosis, it interferes with the complex enzyme reactions involved in energy production for exercise and creates wild fluctuations in the blood sugar level. You'll feel great for awhile, terrible later if you don't get home real fast. A bag of dates, raisins, orange slices, dried apricots and bananas is your best bet for energy and refreshment.

Take an extra set of socks and underwear. A change of socks and shorts about three-quarters of the way through a long ride is the next-best thing to getting a new set of legs.

Don't forget the distance cyclist's greatest friend and one of the best-kept secrets in the sport: a 6" x 6" kitchen sponge. During the first half of your ride you can wet it down with your water bottle and cool your face, neck, shoulders, arms and legs. Aaaah! And on the way home you can stuff it in your shorts and ride in Scenicruiser comfort. Aaaaah! Doesn't look normal when you stand up at stoplights, but by then you won't care. In endurance feats of cycling performance, the gold medal goes to the part that comes off the saddle last.

Carry only necessities. Unless you're returning the next day, mail things ahead. Unfortunately, these days the cyclist travels faster than the US mail. Be sure to send things far enough ahead that they arrive before you do. "Necessity" is hard to define. Why not be self-sufficient? Take everything to fix anything on your bike, including spare cables, brake blocks, a new tube or sewup tire to avoid fixing flats at roadside, cotterless crank tool, chain breaker, extra spokes, freewheel tool, etc.

Bike shops aren't usually open on Sunday. If you're riding in a group, share tools and spares.

Insect repellent is imperative. Get *only* the best. Some kinds just simply do not work. Cutters is super good in the liquid form. So is Repel. Woodsman's Fly Dope is legendary; if you can't get it locally, order from EMS, 1041 Commonwealth Avenue, Boston, Mass. 02215. Cutters probably lasts longest. There's also a fantastic army surplus bug repellent, a yellow liquid that comes in little glass bottles. A hiker in the Sierras encountered devastating swarms of mosquitoes while using this stuff and wasn't bitten once anywhere he'd applied it. Others on the same trail were being eaten alive while using fancy spray repellents.

Groups should travel with the weakest rider taking the lead, the strongest at the rear, unless you've agreed to split up and meet at the end of the day. In that case, take your own tools. *Never* overlap your front wheel with the back wheel of the rider ahead. One slight touch of wheels and he's unaffected, while you will with 100% certainty, be dumped—very hard—right onto the pavement. When facing a headwind, take turns pulling at the front with the rest of the group riding in the leader's wind shadow as racers do. Establish a fixed pattern of switching off, the lead rider pulling over a couple of feet to the left after looking behind to check traffic, then falling back to the end of the line. Don't fall so far back that you have to "jump" to "get back on," which wastes energy.

This is a good place to remind you that all cyclists have a vested interest in preserving their right to an equal share of the road with automobiles. This means that you ride as a *vehicle*, and not as a toy bicyclist or inferior "guest" on the highway. Ride with consideration for automobile drivers and for yourself. Be visible and predictable. Ride a straight line and signal your moves well in advance. It *is* safe to ride the roads in traffic, if you know what you're doing. Less than 2% of cyclist/auto accidents involve the cyclist being hit from behind—the accident feared most by novice riders. And in most of those cases, the cyclist was riding unpredictably or was hit by a right-hand turning driver because the cyclist had failed to ride to the left of the right-turn lane when approaching an intersection, had forgotten to check to the rear before the intersection, etc. The first time you drove a car in traffic, you were nervous. When you've reached basic traffic cycling competence, you'll ride as safely and confidently as you've learned to drive your car.

Chapter 4

A Greased Cone Lowers The Cost

You would not *believe* how simple bicycle maintenance is. Some people think that if they take the cranks off a bike, the mainspring will break and about a thousand delicate pawls, flywheels, jewels and priceless crystal diodes will fly out, forever ruined. It ain't so. There are a few jobs that are more easily and accurately done, at least at first, by a shop mechanic—truing wheels, spoking rims, replacing headsets, rebuilding freewheels. But if you're smart enough to have read this far and if you've got even modest mechanical ability, you *can* fix your bicycle. Period. All you need is someone to tell you how.

GENERAL PRINCIPLES OF BIKE MECHANICS

Remember Murphy's Law: If anything can go wrong, it will. There are many interesting corollaries, such as:

● If everything seems to be working well, you have probably forgotten something.

● The threads that get stripped will always be on the part most critical for proper functioning of the bicycle. A spare will not be available.

● Any part that is dropped will always roll into the most inaccessible crack. That part is always essential to the functioning of the machine. A spare will not be available.

Before you have finished with bicycles you will have discovered many more. Hopefully, with experience you will be able to thwart Murphy's Laws. One thing about them, though, they are very democratic. There is no discrimination as to race, age, sex, religion, creed or expertise. The best anyone can do is minimize their effects. That's what we will attempt here.

● When things are in proper working order, they make a good *sound*. Some people talk to their plants. There are even people who talk to their bicycles. But the good mechanic is like the good conversationalist: he is a good listener.

● When things are in proper working order, they *feel* good. Learn the sound and feel of things when they are working properly. Up to this point in your life, about 80% of the information you processed came through your eyes. Sight is such a convenience that we often ignore information available from other senses. Very few of the vital parts of the bicycle can be seen when they are functioning. You can't see the ball bearings and cones in the hub for example. You may see how easily the wheel swings freely when suspended by its axle, but it is feel that tells you the system is too loose. It's sound and feel that tell you there's grit in the lubricant.

Notice how beginners shift their rear derailleurs. They invariably *look* to see if they are in the proper gear. The more experienced rider has learned the sound and feel of being on the proper cog. There are more important places to be looking while riding.

● Never force things! Use the smallest tool that will just do the job. One fatal error of beginners is to use an 18-inch wrench where a six-inch is more than adequate. The Mafac tool kit is often criticized because it is difficult to get sufficient torque for some jobs. These little tools are excellent for a start, however, and for carrying with you. From them you can work up to bigger tools as they become necessary.

• Have spare parts on hand or at least wait until supply stores are open before you get too deeply involved.

• Not only do functioning parts sound and feel good, tools also sound and feel good when they are working properly. Expertise will come with time, as long as you do your own work. The klotz was created, not born. If someone else always did the job for you because you shouldn't get dirty, you were too young, too old, weaker, the wrong sex, etc., try it anyway. Liberate yourself! The more you attempt for yourself, the more you will be able to do. Soon you will be helping others.

• Cultivate the habit of being orderly. As parts are removed, lay them out in a systematic pattern. Sketch diagrams of how things relate. Don't worry about not being an artist. Any sketch, no matter how crude, is better than none at all. Keep track of the number of ball bearings that come out of a particular location. It helps to get the same amount back in there again.

• For general orientation, consider the side of the bicycle that is on your right as you ride it the right side of the bike. Make some mark with crayon, magic marker, or tape on the right side of parts that can get turned around.

• When a part has been removed from the right hand side, place it on your right. Place parts in sequence on your right from right to left. Place the side that faces inwards face down. Parts removed from the left side are placed on your left, from left to right, as they are removed. Again, the side down is the side facing inwards.

Some parts are particularly difficult to balance face down, but can be placed over a nail in a board for maintaining proper orientation. It might be helpful to the beginner, if you feel very insecure, to make a board to hold things in place. A 36" x 6" x ½" board with two-inch finishing nails spaced three inches apart should do quite nicely.

• Kerosene is probably the only solvent one should use. *Never* use gasoline of any kind. The explosion and fire hazard is

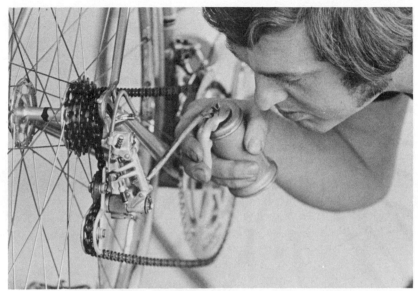

British national team mechanic Steve Aldridge oils a derailleur. Silicon spray's a better choice for utility bikes. (Ted Mock)

much too great and the leaded kind has its own danger—lead poisoning. Avoid smoking anywhere near your work area. Avoid smoking anywhere, lots of people will appreciate it. Always have adequate ventilation where you work. Do not use chlorinated hydrocarbons. Most are deadly and of those that do not seem to be, not enough is known about the long-term effects of their use.

    ● The last part off usually will be the first part back on. After reassembly, if you find parts left over, it just proves Murphy was right. Leftover parts are a no-no! If you didn't read the directions, try it. If that doesn't work by itself, try following them too. Murphy may still win, but if you do not follow a systematic procedure, you rarely will.

    That old saw about cleanliness and godliness applies to bicycle mechanics as well. Keep yourself and all parts clean, at least while putting things back together. It is an exercise in utmost futility to clean all those parts meticulously with toothbrush, kerosene and rags, only to gum them up again with gritty hands.

The following diagram may help to illustrate a systematic approach in removing parts.

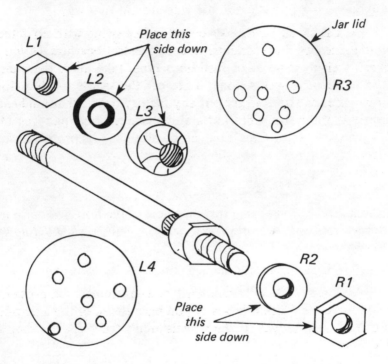

THE NEW BICYCLE

Bike shop mechanics are, on par, more conscientious and honest than auto mechanics; but face it, they're busy. It's not surprising, in a shop that sells perhaps 100 new bikes a month, to find a loose bolt here and there. In some cases, it doesn't make much difference; in others, it's deadly.

● Go over every nut and bolt. The stem expander bolt (aha, look it up!) shouldn't be so tight that your head tube gets to looking like it's swallowed a mouse. But it should be tight enough that the bars and fork don't part company at 30 mph. The seatpost binder bolt shouldn't be tightened so much that the fittings are mashed. If you have cotterless cranks, get a crank tool when you buy the bike; cotterless cranks tend to loosen—you'll ruin them if you ride around that way.

• Check all bearing systems for free swing with no detectable looseness: hubs, cranks, steering headset bearings. If you're the insatiably curious or fastidious type, take apart the cranks just to learn how it's done. Take off the saddle, push a cloth down the seat tube to get out any factory debris that might fall down in the bottom bracket and damage the bearing races. Me, I'd rather be out riding. You can do all this in its proper season, after 1000 miles or so when it's time to regrease your crank bearings.

• Put a little soft solder on the cable ends before they have a chance to become frayed. Check cable housings for burrs at the ends and for proper lubrication. Squirt a little graphite down the ends.

• Check tire inflation.

• Check wheel alignment and—extremely important—make sure the quick releases, if you have them, or the axle nuts, are tight, tight, tight. If the wheels aren't true, ask the shop to fix them.

• Lubricate all external pivot points and wipe off excess lubricant. The shop should have done this, actually, but it's not worth quibbling about. This is a good time to list recommended lubricants and service procedure for the various parts:

Bottom Bracket: Phil Wood or Campagnolo grease; automotive engine assembly and chassis greases are also more than adequate. Avoid very thick greases such as automotive wheel bearing grease, which won't circulate properly on the small bicycle bearings.

Chain: Clean it in solvent, then put it in a container of hot SAE 40 oil (have adequate ventilation!). Let the chain cool, wipe it off and remount it. This is the only way to be sure of getting oil *inside* the chain. You might spray the chain with a commercial chain seal, available at motorcycle shops.

Hub Bearings: The grease used for the bottom bracket is suitable for hubs.

Headset: Use the same grease as for bottom bracket and hubs.

Pedals: Again, use the bottom bracket grease.

Freewheel: The lubricant is sealed in at the time of manufacture, but if your freewheel starts squeaking, a soak in hot SAE 30 or 40 oil will usually eliminate the problem.

Derailleurs: Silicon spray, which picks up less dirt, is a better choice than oil or grease.

Brakes: Calipers and cables should both be lubricated with silicon spray.

Here's a chart that'll tell you how long it's been since you should have done routine lubrication:

Component	Lubricant	Interval
derailleurs	silicon	monthly
brakes	silicon	monthly
chain	oil	3 months
bottom bracket	grease	6 months
hubs	grease	6 months
pedals	grease	6 months
headset	grease	12 months
freewheel	oil	when squeaky

EVERYDAY CHORES

These come under the category of hassle prevention. Take care of it now and it won't stop you out on the road.

● Check tires for trapped glass bits, tread cuts. Use a tread stop compound in the cuts.

● Maintain inflation pressure.

● Keep wheels trued.

• Keep external parts fairly free of dirt, particularly the chain, chainwheels, derailleur and cogs.

• Check all points of cable attachment for fraying and signs of weakness.

• Every 6 months or 1000-2000 miles rotate your (new) spare tire to the front of the bike, front tire to rear, and use the old rear tire as a spare.

BASIC MATERIALS FOR CYCLING MAINTENANCE

To be carried on the bike:

- a high quality six-inch adjustable wrench
- small ignition-type pliers
- small screwdriver—one on pocket knife will do
- tire pressure gauge—0 to 120 lbs
- tire patch kit
- frame-mounted tire pump
- spare tube (or spare tubular tire)
- spoke wrench
- about a foot of brake cable with a firm knot on one end
- chain rivet tool
- small plastic tube of grease or non-detergent oil

With the above equipment, you should be able to take trips in excess of 100 miles and be independent enough so that the only reason you need to pull into a service station is to use the rest room.

Home Base Tools:

- freewheel remover
- set screw or Allen wrenches if applicable
- hammer
- 10- or 12-inch adjustable wrench (1 1/8" or 1 1/4")
- water pump pliers—12"
- pliers with wire cutters
- half-round file
- small punch
- standard and phillips head screw drivers
- tweezers
- cone wrenches—consult shop personnel for proper sizes
- lock ring spanner (Raleigh all-purpose tool)

- cotterless crank tool (if you have cotterless cranks)
- oil cans (squirt gun type makes an excellent grease gun)
- soldering equipment—torch or iron
- if you feel affluent, a set of metric socket wrenches

Miscellaneous:

- roll of duct tape to wrap tool handles; it adds comfort and is most handy for a variety of emergency repairs
- contact cement—an excellent and inexpensive rim cement for tubular tires; carry a tube with you
- tuna fish cans, coffee cans and metal jar lids
- kerosene for cleaning; *do not use gasoline!*
- old tooth brushes
- rags and newspapers
- good hand cleaner

Spare Parts

- brake and shift cables
- assorted ball bearings—1/8", 5/32", 3/16", 1/4"
- extra cotters
- front and rear axle
- brake shoes
- never throw anything away that may be of some use later

An adjustable wrench of poor quality or one used improperly will do irreversible harm to the nuts upon which it is inflicted. Hex nuts sooner or later become cylinders. At this point you resort to pliers which are the pinnacle of brutality. So always tighten the wrench fully before turning.

COMMON MAINTENANCE PROBLEMS AND THEIR TREATMENT

DERAILLEURS:

    a. Front Derailleur

        1. The chain winds off

            i. at random—no special position or number of turns of the cranks

                Solution: Set the shift limiting screw or the position of the cage so that it will not over shift on the side where the chain winds off.

　　　　ii. at every rotation of the cranks with the cranks in the same position

　　　　　　Solution: Look for a bent chainwheel at the point where the chain winds off. Mark the spot and straighten it in a vise.

　　2. Chain rubs on the shift cage

　　　　i. when the chain is on the small chainwheel

　　　　　　Solution: If the rubbing is on the inside face of the cage, adjust the limiting device to move the cage inward.

　　　　　　　　If the rubbing is on the outside face of the cage, pull the shift lever back a bit until the cable clears the chain.

　　　　ii. when the chain is on the largest chainwheel

　　　　　　Solution: If the rubbing is on the inside face, set the limiting screw inward a bit until the cage stays clear.

　　　　　　　　If the rubbing is on the outside face, set the limiting screw so the cage moves out more.

　　3. It will not shift onto a given chainwheel.

　　　　Solution: Take up the cable slack and/or adjust the appropriate limiting screw

　　4. The chain slips on the large chainwheel under stress.

　　　　Solution: Take up the cable slack, look at the chainwheel from the side and press down on the pedal. If you can see under the chain, your chain is worn. Measure its length and compare it to the length when it was new. The chances are it is now almost two inches longer—way past replacement time. New chains only work well with new freewheel cogs.   Grease is cheaper!

　　5. The chain only slips in the small chainwheel, small cog setting.

　　　　Solution: Check the chain tension setting.

b. Rear Derailleur

1. Chain winds off
   i. onto the frame
      Solution: Set the outward limiting screw inward a bit.
   ii. onto the spokes
      Solution: Set the limiting screw inward a bit.
2. Will not shift onto the:
   i. large cog
      Solution: Take up the cable slack and/or the inside limiting screw outward a bit until shifting is possible.
   ii. small cog
      Solution: Clean and lubricate the pivot points and check the outside limiting screw. It may need to come out a bit.

SKIPPING AND SLIPPING OF THE CHAIN

a. for any cog/chainwheel combination at a predictable number of crank revolutions
   Solution: Look for a sticky link in the chain. Remove the tightness with your chain rivet tool. Cleaning and lubrication also may help.
b. only with the smallest cog/chainwheel combination
   Solution: See No. 5 above. Also see if the rear wheel is as far back in the dropouts as it should be.
c. on the largest chainwheel
   Solution: See No. 4 above.
d. at each push on the pedals in any cog/chainwheel combination
   Solution: Check the crank cones, crank cotters, and crank bolts on cotterless cranks. *Do not continue to ride with loose cranks.* It can turn out to be a very expensive trip.

WHEEL RUBS

a. On fork, chain stays or seat stays

Solution: Seat axle properly and tighten axle nuts or quick release

b. On brakes

Solution: True the wheel and/or align brakes.

CHANGE IN SADDLE OR HANDLE BAR POSITION

Solution: Take up on binder bolts and/or shellac stem or seat post.

STEERING

a. Clunking when front brake is applied

Solution: Take up on headset cones.

b. Steering alternately tight and loose as the handle bars are turned through an arc

Solution: The headset has become brinelled. Replace the bearings in the brinelled race with free balls if they were in cages or with the next size larger balls if they were not. Sometimes just shifting one race slightly will also help. Otherwise replace the head set.

BRAKES

a. Too much travel

Solutions:

a. Take up cable slack with the thumb screw.
b. Return thumb screw to lowest position and take up slack at the binder belt.
c. Rotate the brake shoes. Be sure the closed end is still forward.
d. Rotate the rear brake shoes to the front and front to rear.

b. Sticking

Solutions:

a. Lubricate all pivot points.
b. Check housing for burrs.
c. Check for fraying.
d. Lubricate housings.

e. Check alignment of parts—particularly on rear center pull brakes at
the seat post.

TIRE CARE AND REPAIR

The kindest thing you can do for your tires is to inflate them properly. A nylon cord tire that can be inflated to 65 pounds per square inch will last 5000 to 6000 miles unless you get a serious glass cut. Under-inflation leads to excess flexing of the cord, which causes fatigue and premature failure. Over-inflation may tax the strength of the fibers and lead to a dangerous blowout.

In general, the greater your weight and/or the weight you intend to carry, the higher the inflation pressure rating should be. Regardless of your weight, the higher the inflation pressure the lower the rolling resistance. However, if the road surface is extremely rough, much of your pedaling energy will be consumed in moving up and down rather than forward. There exists a compromise somewhere between the maximum pressure, your own weight, and the road surface conditions.

PUNCTURES

If you know the location of a puncture, it is not necessary to remove the wheel to make a repair. If you can find the puncture point without looking at the tube, try this system:

● Turn the bike upside down and lay it on its side.

● Locate the puncture and remove the offending object if it is still present.

● With a tire iron or blunt screwdriver, pry the tire off the rim.

● Pull out the tube in the area of the puncture and patch according to the directions that come with the cold patch kit. The major points to observe are the roughing of the surface and not to get dirty fingers on the tube or fresh surface of the patch.

● Push the patched tube back in place and with your

thumbs and a blunt tire iron, force the tire back on the rim. Don't pinch the tube!

● After the tire is in place again, beat on it with the handle of a screwdriver or wrench. This will help free the tube of folds which may cause further puncture upon reinflation. Slightly inflate the tire and repeat the pounding. Then fully inflate.

If you do not know the location of the puncture or the reason for a flat tire, attempt to reinflate it first. Some joker may have simply let the air out. Place a drop of saliva on the valve and see if it bubbles. One nasty way to let the air out of a tire is to just slightly loosen the valve core. Retighten the valve core and test again. Some valve caps come with a little slotted tool for this purpose. No leak now? Good. You're on your way. Still goes flat? Now you do have a problem.

● Remove the wheel.

● Remove the tire completely.

● Partly inflate the tube and immerse it in a container of water. The trail of little bubbles will show you where the hole is located.

● Patch as before and replace the tube in the tire.

● Work the tire into the rim, one side at a time. A little talcum powder on the tube and tire makes the process easier and helps the tube settle without getting pinched.

● Repeat the beating of the tire as discussed above and reinflate.

Tubular tires present a few more problems in repair than clinchers, but the actual repair of the tube is the same; the patches are just thinner. Opening up and resewing rubberized canvas is a hassle but it is the price you pay for less rotating mass and the convenience of quick changes on the road. There are many excellent references on tubular repair. It really isn't all that bad. But it does take longer.

It is most important to cement tubulars (or sewups, if you

prefer) securely to the rim. A blown tire wrapping itself about your axle at high speed can lead to some ultra-fancy ballet-like maneuvering. It is one thrill you can live without.

For economy, ordinary rubber cement used for gluing paper works quite well in holding the chafing tape over the stitching. Contact cements make excellent rim cements. In fact, they almost hold too well. "Plastic rubber" such as made by Duro makes an excellent tread stopping compound.

The longevity of tubulars, in my experience, is inversely proportional to the number of slobs in a given area who insist on breaking bottles on the roadway. It should be most interesting to gather statistics before and after anti-disposable container laws are passed. I have an ample supply of the "before" data. I would be most happy to also collect the "after" data, should our beloved legislators ever choose to pass such a law.

Much tubular failure is due to the rotting of the cord where water has entered tread cuts. I have taken to treating my tubulars with Cuprinol, a wood preservative. It will be interesting to see if I can wear out a tubular before it rots. *Never* put a tubular into a waterproof container. You will be amazed at how fast cotton rots.

FRONT HUB MAINTENANCE

Judging by the stock of spare parts available, it would appear that hubs are the most frequently abused and repaired system on a bicycle after tires.

Mastery of the mechanics of this system is basic to mastery of all other bearing-supported systems on the bicycle. The pedals might have been an easier place to start. However, so many less-expensive models now come equipped with "throwaway" nonadjustable pedals that one cannot rely on everyone having a decent pair to learn from. The headset of the steering column, the cranks, pedals, freewheel and rear hub are all parallel in design and adjustment.

• Basic orientation: Parts on your right as you sit in the riding position will be referred to as the right-hand parts. Mark the right side of your hub with magic marker, crayon or tape.

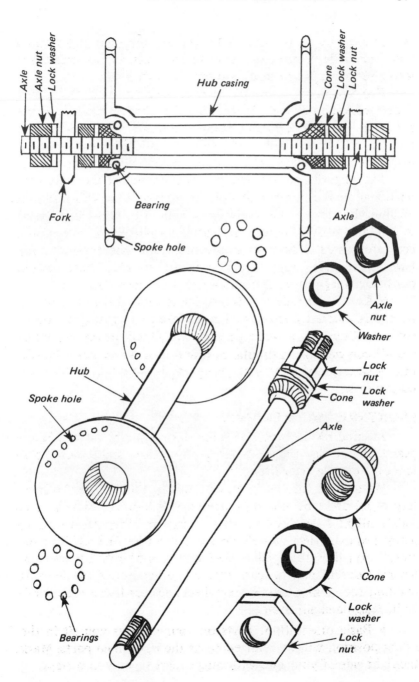

Axle
Axle nut
Lock washer
Hub casing
Cone
Lock washer
Lock nut

Fork
Bearing
Spoke hole
Axle

Hub
Spoke hole

Axle nut
Washer

Lock nut
Lock washer
Cone

Axle

Cone

Lock washer

Lock nut

Bearings

● Before proceeding, be sure you have read the General Principles section.

● Remove the front wheel. Place your adjustable wrench on the right axle nut. Tighten the wrench jaws firmly onto the flat sides of this nut and rotate the nut *counter*clockwise. (Left is loose.) If the nut will not budge, move your hand further toward the end of the wrench handle. If that doesn't help, stand so that the mass of your body is over the wrench handle and lean on it as you turn. Still no go? Add a few drops of liquid wrench and try the left axle nut. If all else fails, get a bigger wrench. Be sure you know which way is counterclockwise.

● After you have removed your front wheel, remove the nuts and washers that held the wheel in place and position them systematically right and left as indicated under General Principles.

● With your cone wrench on the right cone and your adjustable wrench on the left cone lock nut, turn the lock nut left (counterclockwise) and remove it. Place it in the proper position and sequence in your systematic plan. Remove the lock washer and place in the sequence.

● Place the wheel right side down on a flat surface and remove the left hand cone. Support the axle at the right end so it won't drop out of the hub amid a shower of bearings. Place a small jar lid to the right of the cone and put the left-hand bearings in this lid. Count them and write the number down.

● Support the axle at the right and place a rag under the hub to catch any bearings that might drop out. Lay the wheel flat on this rag and remove the right-hand bearings to another jar lid. Lift out the axle-right-hand-cone assembly and set it in its proper sequence.

● Proceed through your sequence of parts from one end to the other and wipe each part clean with a rag. Clean each part with toothbrush and kerosene and wipe dry with a clean rag.

If your hub system has an integral cone lock nut—that is, it is one part, not three—omit step three above. Leave the right

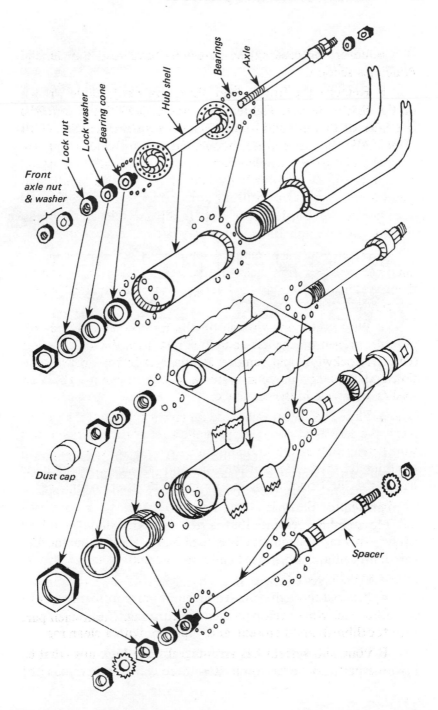

Bearings

Axle

Hub shell

Bearing cone

Lock washer

Lock nut

Front
axle nut
& washer

Dust cap

Spacer

cone undisturbed throughout, once you have seen to it that equal amounts of axle protrude from the hub. Skip step 5 and proceed through step 9. *Do not remove that right-hand cone.*

● Examine your cones and ball cups carefully for pits, chips and irregular wear. Often irregular wear will self-correct if the assembly is run properly adjusted for a while. Severely pitted and chipped cones should be replaced.

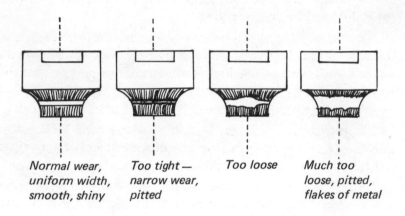

| Normal wear, uniform width, smooth, shiny | Too tight — narrow wear, pitted | Too loose | Much too loose, pitted, flakes of metal |

In the first three cases above, left to right, the situation will self-correct through normal wear after proper adjustment. In the case at the right, the cone should be replaced. Also replace worn and pitted bearings.

Reassembly is essentially the reverse of disassembly. If you have followed a systematic layout of parts, start from the last part removed and work backwards.

● Put a layer of grease in each ball cup of the hub comparable to the bead of tooth paste you put on your brush in the morning. For winter riding, add a few drops of oil to each ball cup.

● Place the wheel on a flat surface, left side down. Insert the bearings with your tweezers. Add a layer of grease over the bearings and smear some on the right-hand bearing cone. Insert the axle.

• Raise the wheel vertically upwards so that the axle drops into place on the bearings. Support the axle in place with one hand and invert the system. Return the wheel to a flat surface and rest it on the axle end.

• Replace the left hand bearings and cover them with a light layer of grease.

• Grease the left cone and turn it down to the bearings. Add a little oil for winter riding.

• Replace the lock washer and lock nut. A little grease on the axle threads is advised. If your machine does not come with separate lock washer and lock nut, you are ready to replace the wheel into the fork-end dropouts.

Now comes the tricky part. These next steps are critical!

• If you have a cone, lock washer and cone lock nut as three separate pieces, turn the cone down to barely finger tight and the lock nut to finger tight.

• Grasp the ends of the axle and try to move it sideways in the wheel. If any looseness is detected, tighten the cone and lock nut a hair. This means *any* looseness. This is based on what you can *feel*, not on what you can see. If you can see it move, it really is loose. The totally blind can become skilled mechanics— most good mechanical adjustments are done by how things feel and sound, not how they look. The difference between a cone that is properly adjusted and one that is too loose may be a thousandth of an inch or less. It is just not practical to try and *see* that.

• When the axle seems free of looseness, place the tire valve at the 3 or 9 o'clock position and support the axle ends on the tips of your forefingers. The wheel should swing down from 3 o'clock, past 6 and up past 7 or 8, and then swing back past six and possibly through 5 and so on. If it stops abruptly after the first pass through 6, things are too tight. Also, if the axle rolls on your fingertips, it is too tight. In some cases irregular wear will cause the system to be too tight on one try, but if the axle is given ¼- to ½-turn it will swing freely. In such a case, quit while you are ahead. Ride a few hundred miles and try again. It may self-correct as things break in.

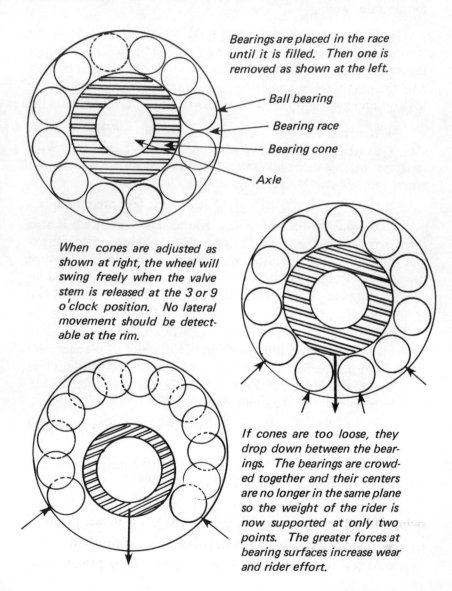

Bearings are placed in the race until it is filled. Then one is removed as shown at the left.

— Ball bearing

— Bearing race

— Bearing cone

— Axle

When cones are adjusted as shown at right, the wheel will swing freely when the valve stem is released at the 3 or 9 o'clock position. No lateral movement should be detectable at the rim.

If cones are too loose, they drop down between the bearings. The bearings are crowded together and their centers are no longer in the same plane so the weight of the rider is now supported at only two points. The greater forces at bearing surfaces increase wear and rider effort.

● If the cones were too tight, put a cone wrench on each cone. Hold the right cone stationary and turn the left one counterclockwise about 1/8-turn. Repeat the swing test. Readjust until the system swings as it should. Give the shake test for looseness as well.

● If looseness is detected, hold the right cone lock nut stationary and turn the left cone clockwise by half the amount it was loosened. If it becomes too tight, loosen again, but for half the amount the cone was just tightened. Repeat tightening and loosening by half amounts until you get a perfect free swing and no looseness.

● Finally, hold the left cone stationary and turn the lock nut tight against it. Now replace the wheel in the fork, align the wheel and tighten the axle nut securely.

● Make the swing test again. On some cheaper models the stressing and compression of the axle in the forkends will also compress the bearing cones. If this is the case, loosen the left axle nuts about ½-turn. Loosen the cone lock nut 1/8- to 1/4-turn. Back out the cone a hair to 1/8-turn, hold it stationary and retighten the cone lock nut and axle nut in that order. Give it the swing test again. If it is still too tight, back out the cone as above by another 1/8-turn. Again, you *feel* for looseness. If you detect looseness, tighten by half the amount that you last loosened it. If it becomes too tight, loosen by half that amount.

If your hub cones were one piece, replace the system in the fork and tighten the right-hand axle nut firmly.

● Tighten the left cone to barely finger tight so that the axle still swings freely.

● Align the wheel in the fork and tighten the left axle nut securely enough to hold the wheel in position.

● Test for looseness at the rim by feel and test for free swing. If both tests are passed, tighten the left axle nut firmly.

● Test for free swing. If this is OK, you are finished.

● If the system fails the free swing test, loosen the left axle nut ¼-turn. Loosen the cone 1/8-turn. Tighten the axle nut and test for free swing and looseness.

● Repeat the loosening and tightening by half increments until there is no looseness and the wheel swings freely.

You are now on the way to becoming a fairly decent mechanic. Once you have mastered the art of the front hub, the rest of the bearing systems on your bicycle will seem less formidable. Of course coaster brakes, three-speed hubs and some freewheels have a few other goodies thrown in to confuse things a bit, but cone adjustment is basically the same in cranks, pedals and headsets.

CRANKS

Ashtabula cranks or one-piece cranks (contemptuously known as American cotterless) are about the easiest to work with, but they are the heaviest on the market. Removing cotters from cottered cranks can be a real chore. A drop or two of liquid wrench a day or so before you work on them may be helpful. Also make sure that you have some spares handy. Occasionally they have to be drilled out.

Some bike shops have a large, expensive tool that makes cotter pin removal relatively easy. Why not just wail on the stupid thing with a hammer? This is definitely the wrong thing to do, as the force of each blow is transmitted to the crank axle bearings, and makes little indentations in the bearing races. Here's an easy solution to the problem:

A piece of two-by-four long enough to support the crank arm and axle will be most helpful. Drill a hole in one end that is wide and deep enough to receive the cotter. With one end of this block on a firmly supported floor and the other supporting the crank with the cotter over the hole, loosen the cotter nut a bit. Place a nail set punch centered on the cotter and tap firmly. Remove the nut completely and tap the cotter out. If it didn't budge the first time, you have a problem. Get that spare cotter handy. Get a bigger hammer, hit harder,   bang hell out of it, swear, pray, etc. By now you have a nice dent in the cotter, so if it hasn't budged, get a drill about 1/16" smaller than the cotter and start drilling. Periodically give the thing a rap with the punch.

When you replace the cotter, liberally apply grease to all surfaces involved. Next time it may not be such a problem. Do not try to pull the cotter through with the nut. Tap it through with a light hammer and then tighten the nut. Tap again and check the nut for looseness. When the nut isn't loosening at each tap, you have finished. Check for looseness periodically. Stop riding and tighten things up anytime you detect looseness.

For details of coaster brakes and in-the-hub shifters, check a more detailed source such as Glenn's or Sincere's manuals.

Derailleurs can be removed intact and given the toothbrush/kerosene treatment. A trip to your local gas station air pump may be helpful. You will be amazed at what you can blow out of that thing. You will be amazed at the mess it can make of a white shirt, too.

THE THREE-SPEED HUB

This is one of those areas that you are usually told to leave to the experts. However, it is rare that anything is really wrong with a three-speed that needs taking apart to fix. The trouble can almost always be traced to stretching of the shift cable.

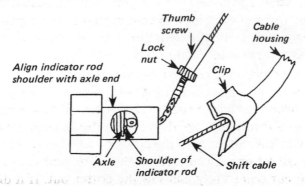

If you place the shift in its middle position, check that hole in the right-hand axle nut. It was put there to tell you something. When the shift is in the 2 position of one marked 1, 2, 3

or the N position of one marked H, N, L, the shoulder of that little rod that enters the axle end should be lined up at the end of the axle. The hole in the side is there so you can see all this.

If the indicator rod is not properly aligned, take up the cable slack at the thumb screw. If there is still too much slack, back off the thumb screw until only three or four threads are engaged. Set the shift lever full forward to give maximum slack to the cable. Trace the cable from the axle back to where it enters a housing at the frame. Loosen the nut that holds this cable housing to the frame and slide it forward until all the slack is gone. Retighten the nut and bolt. Set the shift lever in mid-position and check the alignment of the rod shoulder lever. Set this with the thumb screw. Now it should shift properly in all three gears.

If you are curious and still wish to take the hub apart, go ahead. A good reference is "How to Fix Your Bicycle," for $3.95 from World Publications, Box 366, Mt. View, CA 94040.

FREEWHEEL MAINTENANCE

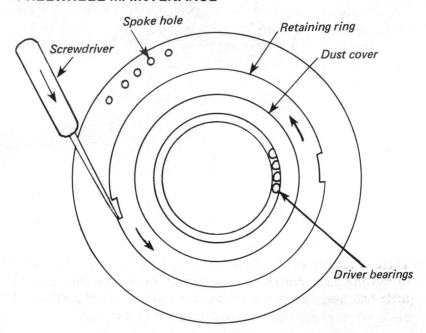

The freewheel is most easily maintained when it has been removed from the hub with the proper tool. Without this specialized tool, freewheel removal becomes major surgery. If you break a spoke on the freewheel side, spoke replacement also becomes major surgery.

Most literature does not recommend amateur freewheel overhaul: "Take it to a reputable bike shop. Let a pro do it." Nonsense. How do you think the pro learned what he knows? If you were not somewhat adventurous, you wouldn't be riding a bicycle in the first place. Have courage, review those general principles and your experience with the front hub, and go ahead.

The first snag you'll hit is the lock ring that holds everything together. That's the thing with the brand name on it, like Atom, Regina, Cyclo or 3.3.3, etc. Also, there will be two shallow little holes drilled on the face of the ring. Remember the "right makes tight, left is loose" principle? Well here is an exception. In this case a clockwise turn removes the ring.

There is reason for this contradiction. Were it not so, the action of moving parts during coasting would loosen the ring, and 88 little ball bearings, pawls, springs and spacers would dribble out along the roadway. Enough can go wrong as it is.

The lock ring can be removed several ways. One way requires an expensive tool. Or, you can attempt to make a tool of your own. Get a piece of hardwood flooring or some equally tough wood. Mark the spacing of the two dents in the face of the lock ring on the wood and drill two pilot holes with this spacing. Take two nails about the diameter of one of the holes on the lock ring face and drive these through the pilot holes. Cut the ends off the nails so that they protrude just a little farther than necessary to engage the holes on the lock ring. File the ends square. If there is enough room, a hole may be drilled between the nails, through which the axle can pass.

The other alternative is to loosen the lock ring with a punch. Set the right-hand dent at 3 o'clock. Set a punch at 45° or more in the dent and strike towards 6 o'clock. Repeat until the ring can be turned by hand. You may have to give up and buy or build a tool—freewheel lock rings are *tight*.

Now the fun begins. Place the wheel freewheel side up on a flat surface. Follow the systematic procedure of the General Principles section. Remove the lock ring and set it to the right. Place the bearings in a jar lid. Keep count. Next remove the thin spacers. In some types, the pawls and return springs can also be removed. If not, hold the freewheel in place and invert the wheel. Have a rag underneath to catch anything that comes cascading out. Carefully raise the wheel away from the cog cluster. Place the pawls in a jar lid and the bearings in another. Count them as usual.

Wrap the freewheel body—still attached to the hub—in a rag and turn it counterclockwise with a large set of pliers. Take care not to grasp this in such a way that the thinner parts are placed under stress.

Clean everything the usual way with toothbrush and kerosene. Clean up the hub and hub threads as well as the threads on the freewheel body. Grease these threads thoroughly and wipe out the excess. It came apart relatively easy, didn't it? Now we'll find out why it's supposed to be left to the experts.

Some recommend only light oil for freewheels. Certainly for the pawls, grease can become a problem, particularly in cold weather. For the beginner at this task, I recommend using grease because it helps to hold things in place during reassembly. If you don't like grease, you can always soak the system in kerosene and oil it after everything is back together again.

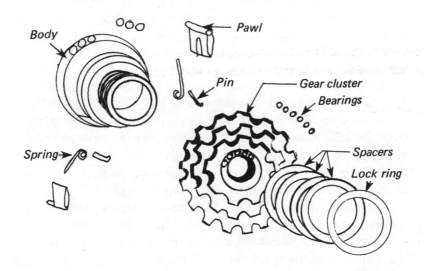

● Set the pawls in their places with their return springs behind them. Take about a foot or so of thread (nylon is best) and strap this around the pawls to hold them in place when lowering the body back into the cog cluster.

● Grease the innermost bearing race and tweeze the balls into place. Carefully lower the body onto the bearings. When it is in place, remove the thread with a pulling, unwinding motion.

● Hold the two parts together and invert carefully.

● Grease the bearing race and replace the balls.

● Replace spacers and turn the lock ring counterclockwise.

If you wish to make the system a little tighter leave out the thinnest spacer for the first try.

Now you are ready to put the freewheel back onto the hub. This must be done with caution and only with your fingers. The tough steel threads of the freewheel body love to devour aluminum alloy hub threads. The new threads that are cut never seem to be as good as the originals. Your fingers will tell you if things are going as they should.

You must also use caution when purchasing a new freewheel. There are some very subtle thread differences between hubs and freewheel bodies. Take your hub with you to the dealer; or if ordering by mail, be sure to specify all the details you have available as to the hub and the brand of freewheel now on that hub.

If you have chewed up your hub threads and cannot afford a new one or the time to rebuild the wheel, you can sometimes get by with a dose of Locktite or one of the cyanoacrilate glues on the market. Take great care with the superglues and have some acetone (nail polish remover) on hand when you use them. They can bond your flesh to anything handy in a few seconds. A good bicyclist is said to form a single entity with his bike, but this is ridiculous. There is nothing humorous about having to be surgically separated from one's freewheel.

Occasionally the pawl return springs will wear out. Take the remains of the spring to your music store or a friend who plays the violin. Fine musical instrument strings can easily be shaped and cut into a perfect replacement. One such string can keep you and your friends in business for quite a while.

WHEEL BUILDING

This is another one of those tasks, the folklore of which makes it seem more difficult than it really is. The method outlined here differs a bit from other published methods but it works. Its success will depend on how reliably you can sketch the required diagrams. If the diagram is in error, your wheel may be all wrong.

Why in the world would anyone want to do this task in the first place? Well, you may be able to salvage a dented or bent rim. You may have to replace a damaged hub. You may wish to convert your present wheels from tubulars to clinchers or vice versa. To some it's like climbing a mountain—it's there and it hasn't been clumb before.

● A day or so before you begin, put a small drop of liquid wrench at the juncture of each spoke and nipple. Rain, salt and road grit may have fused them over the years. It may be wise to have a few extras on hand, as occasionally the only way a spoke can be removed is to cut it.

● Mark the right side of your rim with tape. Also mark the right side of the hub.

● Place the wheel on a table with the left side down and the valve at 12 o'clock. Pay particular attention to the two spokes on the right-hand side of the wheel that are on either side of the valve. They are almost parallel to each other and enter the hub flange tangentially. This key pair will henceforth be referred to as the *parallel pair*. Check the diagrams and note which case matches your wheel:

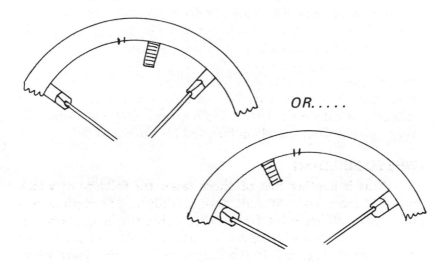

OR.....

● Note the hub flange between the parallel pair of spokes. Exactly how many spokes enter the hub flange between the parallel pair (but not including the parallel pair)? Also note which member of the parallel pair is head up and which is head down through the hub flange. Diagram these conditions as shown in the example below. This is your survival map through the wil-

derness of wheel building. Without it you will become hopelessly
lost.

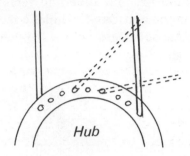

Hub

Review:

- Is the left spoke head of the pair in or out?
- Is the right spoke head in or out?
- How many spokes enter the hub flange between the par-
allel pair? (an even number, I hope—six or eight, usually).

With the left-hand spoke of the parallel pair as a "reference"
at the hub, note that every other spoke in the clockwise direction enters the hub with its head facing the same as the "reference" spoke. At the rim, these alternate spokes have three
spokes between them, one from the right side of the wheel and
two from the left.

Again refer to the left-hand spoke of the parallel pair and
note how many spokes it crosses over (and/or under) on the way
to the rim. Note which spokes it crosses over and which it passes
under. Record this information and then proceed.

- Observe that a spoke that is head down normally passes
over the other spokes on the way to the rim. Occasionally you
will find a case where the last cross nearest the rim is reversed
and the head-down spoke will pass under. The last two crosses
will thus be over and then under, as in weaving. It is more time
consuming to build a wheel this way but some say it distributes
the stresses more uniformly and over a greater number of
spokes. Make note of this so that if such a pattern exists in your

wheel, it will not be lost during the rebuilding process. You may wish to add this form of lacing if you did not originally have it.

● Remove the tire and tube and remove one spoke. Examine the hole in the hub. Are the holes countersunk to distribute the stress of the spoke around the bend at the head? If both sides are countersunk, you have no problem. However, if only one side is countersunk, there is a natural tendency to seat the spoke head into it. Unfortunately, with this orientation a sharp edge rests against the crook of the spoke. Any sudden shock to the wheel gives the spoke a fatal karate chop and off it comes. If you have a tendency to break spokes once a week or so, this may be the reason.

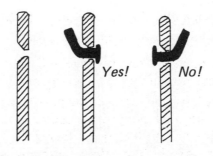

● Start your wheel building experiment with your front wheel. The rear wheel has a subtle aspect to it known as dishing. On some wheels this is accomplished by using shorter spokes on the right-hand side. It may be worthwhile to get into the habit right now, of keeping the right-hand spokes segregated from the left. Dishing is the process of centering the rim between the axle ends as opposed to the hub flanges, when you've got the extra width of the freewheel to work around.

● Loosen all spokes a few turns with the nipple grip (spoke wrench) and the job can be completed with a screwdriver.

● Clean the nipples with a pipe cleaner and kerosene. Dry them well. Fine steel wool and kerosene will restore spokes to their original showroom condition. Clean the threads well.

• Run a greased pipe cleaner through each nipple. Treat the spoke threads to a light coating of grease as well. I have never seen this treatment recommended elsewhere nor have I seen it condemned. The nipples do not seem to work loose, yet future truing is made much easier. It certainly reduces the fusion of nipples and spokes if you ride in winter where much salt is used.

CLOSE YOUR EYES, THINK OF FIELDS OF FLOWERS

Now you are ready to get it all together. Keep calm. No need for you to come apart, too (unless you failed to make those diagrams correctly).

• Place the rim left side down on the table with the valve hole at 12 o'clock.

• Place the hub left side down in the center of the rim.

• Select two right-hand spokes for your parallel pair and insert them according to your diagram. (What? No diagram? Make out a check to your nearest bike shop for $20 and let them build your wheels. You need help!)

• Put the nipples on with four complete turns. Check the orientation of the spoke heads and their position relative to the valve hole. Is the head properly located relative to the countersinking?

• Proceed clockwise from the left member of the parallel pair and insert a spoke into every other hole. Be sure the heads match the position of the head of the reference spoke. Lead each spoke clockwise to every fourth hole in the rim from the reference spoke. Put the nipples on with four complete turns. Watch the cross-over nearest the rim so that it matches the original.

• Insert the remaining right-hand spokes proceeding counterclockwise into the hub and into every other hole in the rim. If you wish, weave the last cross nearest the rim.

• Check your diagrams again. All right-hand spoke holes should be filled and the rim should have a spoke in every other hole.

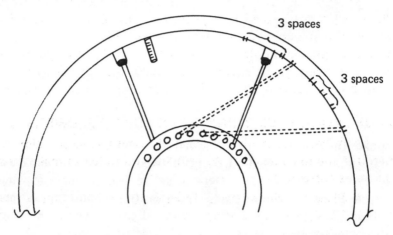

● Turn the wheel left-side up and insert one spoke with its head properly oriented to the countersinking. There also may be a wear groove present as well. Lead this spoke to the rim to the hole that best matches its length. This will be your reference spoke.

● Insert spokes into every other hole in the hub with the same orientation as the reference spoke. Proceed around the rim clockwise from the reference spoke to every fourth hole and put the nipple on with four complete turns.

● Properly orient and insert the remaining spokes and weave the outermost cross or retain the original pattern.

● At this point the wheel should have the consistency of limp spaghetti. If all went well, the spaghetti sticks out uniformly around the rim. If that is not the case—Murphy strikes again!

● Pick the first nipple clockwise from the valve hole and count how many turns it takes to turn it down until only one or two threads are showing. Proceed clockwise around the rim and turn down the remaining nipples the same amount. The wheel should begin to firm up. If not, go around again and give each nipple one complete turn. Continue by complete full turns until the spokes begin to show some tension.

● When the wheel has started to firm up, tighten each nipple only ½- or ¼-turn until the tension approximates the original. (Compare with the left side of the rear wheel.)

WHEEL DISH

If you have done a rear wheel, you're not out of the woods yet. Align the wheel between the chain stays and then look at the situation between the seat stays. Not so hot, is it? Tighten each right-hand spoke one-half turn and loosen each left-hand spoke the same amount. Realign the rim between the chain stays and you will see that things between the seat stays have already begun to improve. Depending on how much the wheel improved and how far you still have to go, continue the process by ½- or ¼-turns until the wheel aligns between both chain stays and the seat stays.

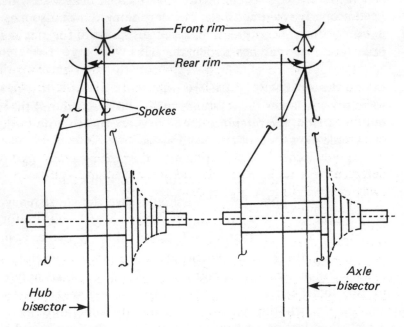

Wrong: Hub-centered rim. Rear wheel does not track along same path as the front wheel.

Right: Dropout-centered rim. "Dished" rear wheel tracks along the path of the front wheel.

CHAIN MAINTENANCE

A healthy chain should be kept clean and dry on the outside but should be well penetrated with lubrication on the inside. Excess lubricant gets thrown down the spokes and onto the rim, tires, derailleurs and frame. Dirt and grit gets carried onto the surface lubricant and the chain becomes a cutting tool wearing down the cogs and chainwheels. Keep the outer surface clean and dry. Pipe cleaners are useful for removing grit from the spaces between the links.

Grease is probably the best lubricant to use but the most difficult to apply with suitable penetration. Properly applied, grease will more than triple the life of a chain when compared to lubrication with oil. Grease dissolved in a volatile solvent penetrates as well as oil. After the solvent evaporates, wipe off the excess external grease. The only trouble is that you can't put a volatile-solvent grease in a pot on the stove for maximum penetration into the chain rollers.

Grease has certain inconveniences. In below-zero weather things can get rather stiff. It is also more difficult to clean a well-greased chain. Use all solvents with great care. The nonflammable solvents are high poisonous and the nonpoisonous (relatively) are usually very flammable or almost explosive.

If you prefer oil, you don't need anything fancy. A nondetergent 40- to 90-SAE oil will serve well and will not wash away in wet riding, as do the detergent oils.

To remove a chain for cleaning, either remove the master link, or if none is present, open the chain with a chain rivet tool. Take care with the chain rivet tool that you do not push the rivet out all the way. If you do, you will have to muster all your patience, luck, skill and expletive incantations to get it back in place again. It is an emotional experience best avoided.

Chain rivet tool directions usually call for turning the rivet driver six full turns. It is more convenient to count half-turns and only push the rivet 11½ half-turns. The small amount of extra rivet not pushed out makes a convenient hook to aid in reassembly.

This is one time when a little diagram of how the chain threads its way through the system will be most helpful. Ease the chain out so that derailleur tension springs do not snap about and get things out of adjustment.

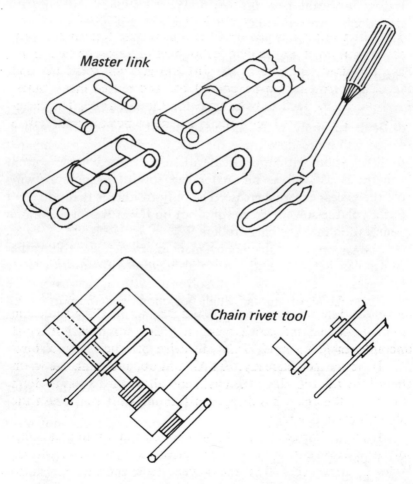

Master link

Chain rivet tool

Removal of chains with master links is shown in the diagram. Push the spring clip forward with a screwdriver at the open end. The rest will come apart with your fingers.

One type of master link only has the side plate, without the spring clip. Just grasp the chain in each hand with the thumbs on either side of the plate. Bend the chain towards the plate and flick the plate off with a finger. At this point you will wish you had three hands, but it will come off.

Soak the dirty chain in just enough kerosene to cover it at the bottom of a coffee can. Scrub thoroughly with a stiff toothbrush. A small bottle brush or coffee pot brush is helpful to get dirt out from between the link plates. Repeat this process several times with only a few ounces of kerosene each time. Save the used kerosene as the dirt and grit will settle out and the clear kerosene can be poured off and reused many times. Fresh kerosene need only be used for the last rinse. The cleaning steps are repeated until the kerosene comes out with only a slight trace of grey tinge.

Next apply a liquid detergent to the chain and again scrub with the brushes. Rinse in warm water and scrub some more. Repeat until no more dirt comes out of the chain. Use the hottest water you can stand or use boiling water and lift the chain out with tongs or pliers. Take the chain outside and swing it over your head to centrifuge out as much water as possible. Take care that you don't get the chain wrapped into your dentures.

Make a final rinse of the chain with acetone or ethanol to remove the last traces of water. Spin dry again. Hang the chain from the ceiling and gently warm it with a torch until it is just uncomfortable to hold. This will drive off the last moisture.

Have warmed oil ready, 90 SAE will do, and dunk the warm chain into the oil. Hang the chain and allow the excess to drain off. After the chain has dripped off about all it can, finish the job with clean dry rags.

If you prefer grease, dunk the warmed chain into grease dissolved in a solvent, about one part grease to three parts solvent. Drain as above and allow the solvent to evaporate. Finish up with the clean dry rags until the exterior surfaces of the chain are clean and dry.

Now that you have gone to so much trouble cleaning that chain, don't profane it by replacing it on dirty cogs and chainwheels. This may seem like just too much, but it will pay off in longer useful chain life. If you ride for the economy involved, you will appreciate not having to buy a new chain any more often than necessary.

Reassembly is just the reverse of disassembly, except that the chain rivet tool mashes things together into one tight lump. Leave about 1/3 to 1/4 of a turn so that the final push can be done on a different chain tool setting to remove this tightness. See the directions that came with your tool.

BRAKE AND SHIFT CABLES

Brake and shift cable housings are one of the biggest problems on machinery from discount sources. The housings are poorly cut and finished and lubrication is often unknown. This latter can be a problem on bikes from some of the better sources.

● Examine the cable ends before removing anything. A frayed, kinked cable may come out of its housing with deceiving ease. Getting things back together is another story.

● Clean the frayed ends with kerosene. Wash with detergent and water. Rinse and dry gently with a torch or soldering iron. Apply soldering flux and flow on some soft solder. Be sure the fraying has been tightly twisted back in place. Trim away any fraying that could not be made smooth.

● Remove the cable from its housing. Clean in kerosene and bend out any kinks. Apply a heavy layer of light grease and set the cable aside.

● Examine the ends of the cable housings. A poorly-cut housing will have a hooked little burr on it that interferes with the smooth action of the cable.

● File the ends of the housing smooth and flat.

● If available, use a countersink, reamer, or tapered rotary file to bevel the inside edges of the housing.

● Force grease through the cable housing. The pump-type oil can makes an excellent grease gun for this. If that is not available, run the greased cable through the housing. Regrease the cable and repeat several times.

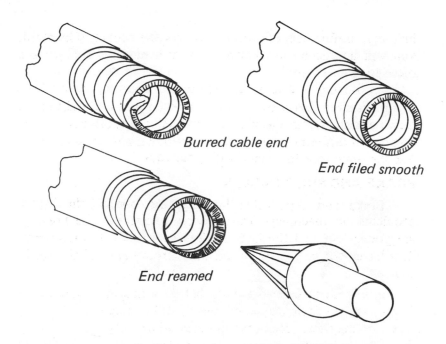

Burred cable end

End filed smooth

End reamed

● Apply grease to all openings through which the cable passes. Now you are ready for reassembly.

● When you have done all the adjustments and taken up all unnecessary slack, do *not* trim off the excess cable. Bend this into a gentle loop and tape the loose end. This excess may be just the amount you'll need to make an emergency repair. Cables most often break off at the lever end. In such an event, loosen the cable retaining nut and pull the cable forward through the housing until the extra cable is all taken up. Put a tight knot at the broken end and insert this knot into the appropriate slot in the brake lever. Take up the slack in the cable and re-tighten the cable retaining bolt.

● Another emergency repair can be done by carrying a suitable length of cable with a knot at one end. Carry the extra cable in your handlebar or taped to your top tube. Save the longer rear brake and derailleur cables when they break for replacing the shorter front brake and shifter cables.

● Most of the better shift and brake systems have a thumb

screw adjustment to take up the slack as cables begin to stretch. Sooner or later this system reaches its limit and the cable must be pulled through the hard way. Turn the thumb screw down to its lowest position. Bind the brake shoes to the rim with several turns of cord and pull up the slack in the cable. There is usually enough slack left in the system so that the brake shoes will be the proper distance from the rim when the cord is removed.

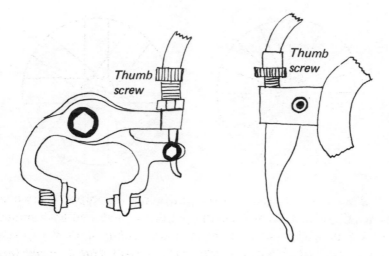

● After taking up the slack in the system and adjusting the brake shoe distance, you may find that the wheel needs truing.

● Before truing your wheel, see that your hub cones are properly adjusted. See the sections on front hub maintenance and truing wheels.

TRUING WHEELS

From time to time your wheels will develop wiggles and wobbles from hitting rocks, chuck holes and the just plain lousy roads in your area. Removing those wobbles and making the rim round again is a process known as truing.

Wheel truing has acquired a mystique that makes it appear very difficult. Actually, you can learn the basics in about five minutes. With a little experience you will be able to twiddle a nipple grip with the experts.

At first sight, a bicycle wheel is a confusing array because of the criss-cross pattern of spokes that gives the wheel its strength. If the spokes ran directly in a line from the hub to the rim, things would be less confusing. For some special purposes, there are such radially-spoked wheels. Your wheels are most likely tangentially-spoked. In tangential spoking, the spoke attaches tangent to the hub flange.

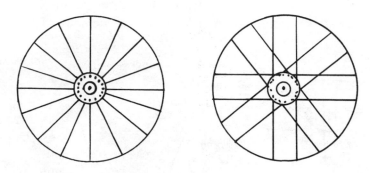

The two patterns on the right below are important when truing the wheel. Note that the pattern is matched by a similar pair on the other side of the hub. *In dealing with the spokes on one side of the wheel, one must always deal in some way with the matching ones nearest to them on the other side of the wheel.*

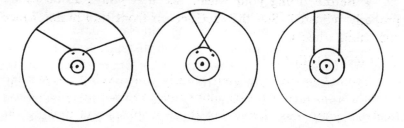

Spokes have right-handed threads, that is, *right makes tight.* This means that if you are working on the tire side of the rim, you would turn the nipple clockwise to tighten the spoke. Most truing can be done with the tire in place, working from the hub

side of the rim.   From this viewpoint, *left makes tight.*
   Be sure that your hub cones are properly adjusted *before*
you proceed. Also, put a drop of liquid wrench at the junction
of the spoke and the nipple. Otherwise you may end up merely
twisting a spoke rather than turning the nipple on the spoke
threads. When the load on the wheel shifts during riding, the
spoke will unwind again and the total effect is zero.
   The diagrams below illustrate how tightening and loosening
various spoke combinations affects the movement of the rim:

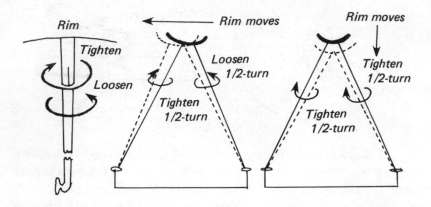

   The brake shoe makes a suitable reference for removing a
side-to-side wobble. Move one shoe up close to the rim and rotate the wheel once. At those points where the rim hits the
shoe, tighten the opposite spoke one-half turn and loosen the
sister spoke (on the brake shoe side) the same amount. Repeat
the process until the rim is a uniform distance from the brake
shoe all the way around. Move the other brake shoe up to the
rim and repeat the truing process for that side of the rim.
   Flats and high points should be fixed with the tire removed.
An improperly seated tire can create highs and lows of its
own. Deal with the high spots first, bringing them down by
tightening spokes on both sides of the rim. Locate the highs
by slowly lowering a magic marker down onto the rotating
rim so that the marker barely flicks at the high spots. Tighten
up the appropriate spokes by half turns (or less). Then remove

your marks with a rag. Repeat until the highs are gone. Loosen at any low spots that remain.

To do a more precise job requires special equipment. For the home tinkerer, see *Bike World*, March 1974, April 1974, and January 1975.

Rip - Proofing Your Bike

Bikes have been stolen in just about every way imaginable. They've been hoisted over 12-foot fences and sawed from their moorings in broad daylight. Whole bike racks have been lifted into trucks with a dozen bikes attached. A leading northern California racer had so many superbikes, each costing over $500, stolen from his high-security house that he just gave up, moved, and took out an unlisted phone number.

Bike theft is one of the easiest games in crime. There is no way you can prevent it. Absolutely no way. The determined thief will succeed, given time and suitable conditions.

The only thing, then, that you can do is to slow the thief down and create uninviting conditions.

• If you ride a superbike, get a "trashmo" for around-town riding. Never let your phone number or address be spread around in cycling circles. Many professional thieves operate with racing and touring informants.

• Park your bike in a conspicuous spot. An anonymous 16-year-old Chicago bike thief stated to a newspaper reporter that he'd been accosted by passers-by while attacking a bike chain with bolt cutters on a main street in broad daylight. He'd calmly told them, "I lost my key, so I had to borrow some bolt cutters to get my bike home." They left him to work undisturbed. Rather discouraging, isn't it? But if your bike is a trashmo, or looks terrible, chances are it won't be worth the thief's effort. Park it next to someone else's Colnago.

● Obviously, keep an eye on the bike as much as possible. Park it within sight from inside stores—*locked!* The fastest human being is no match for the average bike rider, much less a scared one. Many thieves will avoid personal confrontation, but don't count on it. There are sociopaths walking around of whom psychiatrists know that they have not the slightest vestiges of moral compunction. These sick people would just as soon bash your head in as shake your hand if you're in their way. Measure the man, but be prepared to back down if the stakes rise beyond the price of another bicycle.

Looks formidable, doesn't it? In less than 90 seconds, a "good" thief would be riding away on this bike. (Ed Miller photo)

● Components are easy to steal. It takes professional road racing mechanics only a few seconds to change a wheel. Thieves are good at it, too, especially when a quick release hub makes it that much easier. Pass your chain through both wheels and the main frame triangle. Or take the front wheel with you.

● No lock, chain or cable is theft*proof.* One lock ad says, "damages the jaws of bolt cutters." True, but does it prevent the bolt cutters from cutting the lock? What's a $15 pair of bolt cutters compared to a $150 bike?

Two common devices available to the general public will do the job on just about anything sold for security. One is the freon cocktail chiller, and the other is a pocket-sized butane/oxygen torch. The freon chills steel to the point where it becomes brittle and can be shattered by a hammer blow. If the torch doesn't cut directly, it certainly will destroy the hardened qualities of the lock so that other devices will finish the job.

Terms such as alloy steel, hardened steel, and aircraft cable are relatively meaningless. All steel is an alloy of some kind, and all steel is hardened to some degree. The type of hardening process is what is important—through-hardened rather than case-hardened is the only good thief-staller. Aircraft cable sounds secure, but though cable resists cutters it yields readily to a good hacksaw or anvil and chisel. Remember what you learned in shop class—"The right tool for the job."

Your only real hope is probably a $20+ superlock like the Citadel or Kryptonite, and never leaving your bike alone where it can wander off and leave you. Avoid these items:

● Combination locks. Particularly avoid the kind that have three or four rings. The three-ring type with 10 numbers on each ring can be opened in less than two minutes without tools. I have seen brand name combination locks with 5/16" case-hardened shackles that could be opened by prying off the back with a pen-knife.

● Avoid locks with keys that look like they were stamped out. Get one that is pick-resistant and that has a shackle larger in diameter than the chain it locks. Avoid a lock that is weaker than the chain to which it is attached. Chain must be cut in two places, whereas most locks require only one cut. The thicker the lock or chain, the better. If you double the diameter of a chain, it takes four times as long to cut it. Triple the diameter and it takes nine times as long.

● Avoid mild steel. Case hardened is better. Hardened throughout is best.

● Never leave your bike unlocked. Not even for five seconds. If you can't lock it, take it with you. Experienced cyclists will wheel their superbikes into grocery stores, politely asking permission to do so when the manager gives them the evil eye. If a store complains (within reason, you can't expect to take your muddy bike upstairs at Saks Fifth Avenue), cancel your credit, shop elsewhere and write your newspaper action line.

● Lock your bike to something strong. Wrought iron railings are a piece of cheese compared to case-hardened chain. Get a chain long enough to go through both wheels, the frame and around that fixed object.

● Lock the bike to something solid even at home. If you were a burglar in a hurry, which would you take, the $500 TV or the $500 bicycle? Garages and sheds are burglars' retirement homes—their locks are among the poorest and they provide good cover.

● Can you identify your machine? What's the serial number? Do you have it written down? Have a photo on hand. Check the police periodically to see if your stolen bike has been recovered. They're understaffed and often can't notify you if they've found your bike. Frankly, even statewide registration systems are worthless. The first thing a good thief does is to file off the identification numbers on a stolen frame. He can always repaint it and claim it's a hand-built job. If your superbike is stolen, you can just about forget about getting it back—unless the thief is very incompetent.

So, the upshot of it all is that, like the common cold, bike theft is probably here to stay for a long time. The only thing you can do is to up the odds in your favor.

Chapter 5

Goodies for Around-Town Cycling

A very great amount of add-on and replacement gadgetry was invented, re-invented, copied or marketed during the early-'70s surge in bicycle sales. As new bike sales tapered, the gadgeteers gathered momentum. Some of it is useful, some interesting, but not essential, and some new cycling paraphernalia is truly inspired in its functional simplicity.

For fear of unfairly excluding local bike shops and deserving mail order companies, we have listed sources only in cases of hard-to-find items.

In deciding which "goodies" to feature, we asked ourselves which items in each category had stood up under the test of actual year-in, year-out use by high-mileage cyclists. Few long-time cyclists have any use for non–functional gear. Their ideal is not the $2500 rhinestone-studded Cinelli with mink saddle cover which was exhibited at the 1974 New York Bicycle Show.

COMPONENTS

It would require volumes to discuss the relative quality of all the brands and designs of normal bicycle running gear. In this section, we're interested in "add-ons." But the question is inescapable: "Is my Huret derailleur replaceable with Brand X?"

First consider that component switches often involve proper matching of thread standards and other complex factors like the ability of a given derailleur to handle the gearing range you desire, etc. If you ask around among shop mechanics, as we advised in the section on new bikes, you'll get honest accurate advice. Beware, though, the glamor-bitten type who'll arrogantly bray that "If you want to go to cotterless cranks, Campagnolo's the only thing worth considering." It's not true. Get numerous opinions and you'll save money.

At the risk of sounding "age-ist" let's recommend that you question at least one mechanic with a good 20 years of experience. Refer also to the section on "Lightening the Load" and get your priorities straight. For around-town cycling, cotterless cranks and super-derailleurs with racing pedigrees just aren't that important. Valuable changes can, of course, be made where they make a functional difference, such as gearing changes via new cogs or chainwheels; increased comfort by switching saddle, pedals or stem; efficiency improvements like trading steel rims for alloy; throwing away a wretched set of cheap sidepull brakes for inexpensive but superb Mafac centerpulls, and so on.

COMFORT

Oh well, let's go ahead and talk about saddles, even though we just declared them standard running gear. Find out if you like cycling first, before you trade that just-tolerable seat that feels like it was form-fit to someone else's design. If you come to that pleasant state where the thought of driving is irksome, the idea of riding enclosed in a vehicle evoking mild claustrophobic panic—then think about trading saddles.

Test ride a selection of saddles if you can. The old standard is the leather Brooks Professional. It takes many, many miles to break in, whereafter it's dreamy; until then, it's hard as a rock. If you're determined to look like a non-dude even in such niggling details, at least ask around for the latest miracle formula being used to tame this beast.

The Cinelli/Unica nylon-shelled saddles require no break-in, but they don't fit everyone's anatomy as well as might be desired. There are a lot of them around, so try and test ride one—maybe the shop mechanic will let you ride his.

The Ideale saddles from France are leather too, but they're partially broken-in at the factory. The 2002 and the 90IR are excellent. Only trouble is, the factory's softening process leaves a black substance on the saddle which comes off on your clothes for months. We've never tried saddle-soaping it out, but a plastic bag will protect your good clothes, and the black doesn't show on cycling shorts.

"The Seat" is the name of a new saddle being marketed by Cool Gear. Many riders say it's the ultimate in comfort, though a few individuals report they can't conform to this one, either.

Handlebar tape is unexpectedly important. If you ride on ordinary, uncushioned bars, you'll almost certainly experience a feeling of numbness in your hands. This is due to pressure on the ulnar nerve. Continued pressure, as in day-in, day-out riding, can lead to irreversible nerve damage and paralysis. Several solutions exist. One of the best is padded handlebar tape, such as Bailey III tape, or the thick Pro Tour handgrips. You can wrap normal cloth handlebar tape over either for a nicer-feeling grip.

Cycling gloves are a real godsend, definitely not just a silly racers' fetish. If you should fall, they protect your hands from road rash; and the padded palms give added protection to the ulnar nerve. The Gant gloves from France are expensive, but last a very, very long time and give about the best protection available.

Cycling shorts are practical, too. Good shorts are cut so they don't bind up on the legs, they're cool, and they're padded for friction-free, cushioned comfort. How much they'll add to your personal enjoyment depends on how you feel riding your accustomed distances without them. Wool is costlier, nylon shorts like the Emily K brand are durable and well-cut, with a good chamois.

Cycling shoes aren't really necessary for the short-distance cyclist (under 10 miles on average rides). The Italian brands are narrow, the Belgian and German wider, the Mexican shoes seemingly a compromise. Quality is fairly proportional to price. If you're up to paying over $35, the Adidas "Eddy Merckx" model is excellent. Merckx, the world's greatest racing cyclist, sent prototypes back to the factory for design corrections 10 times before he'd allow his name on the shoes.

PUMPS

The Silca Impero is the most commonly-used frame pump for sewup tires. However, the Zefal pumps have better rubber head seals for less leaky action, and the plastic barrel of the Zefal Course model seems to be less liable to cracking than the Silca's. Zefal pumps are also available with Schraeder valve fittings, and a new high-pressure model has a clamp which locks on the valve stem for easier handling.

At this writing a new pump, the "No. 1" marketed by Sketheia and sold in bike shops, was raising eyebrows. It delivers air to the tires on both in- and out-strokes, has a clear plastic barrel, built-in pressure gauge, and is rated at 120 psi. There's no telling yet how durable or accurate it is, but it's worth considering.

Floor pumps, used only at home or taken along in your automobile trunk, are a convenient "extra" because of their ease of operation. Schwinn dealers sell a good one; another is the Medai Super de Luxe with built-in gauge, rated at 140 psi.

JERSEYS

Ah, shucks, hoped you wouldn't ask. This is such a confused area. Some jerseys feel and look great but require very great care in washing; some people prefer nylon, others can't stand the way it feels in hot or cold weather. If you want a really durable, easily-found cycling jersey and expense is no object, get a genuine wool European racing team jersey, for over $25. The Raleigh team jerseys, to give an example, are extremely durable and attractive. The best custom jersey maker in the US is John Kucharik, 17121 So. Western Ave., Gardena, CA.

RAIN GEAR

Ingenuity is the only answer when it starts raining. An unusually ingenious cyclist has designed a really fine rain cape and spats, sold through Belwether and available at many bike shops. Thumb loops keep the cape from blowing up in your face, behind-shoulder flaps keep you from drowning in your own perspiration, and a belt strap keeps the back from flying around. Wet-weather commuters often accept some deficiencies in their "armor" as a fair trade-off for good condensation-free breathability in their clothing. Some commuters keep clean, dry shoes, shirt and pants in a file drawer, cleaning up and changing on arrival and leaving wet clothes in a back room to dry.

If you're faced with cold rain and snow, try a set of Polar Pals toeclip covers. Try your bike shop for them, or write Robert Cartwright, Box 104, West Carrollton, Ohio 45449. Last we heard they were $5.95 a pair, postpaid.

Besides the Polar Pals covers, try rubber-banding plastic bags over your shoes or over your socks. One cyclist has electric socks hooked up to his bike generator.

Fingers are easier to warm than toes. Snowmobile mittens with long cuffs are the greatest.

BIKE BAGS & RACKS

The Swiss-made Pletscher rack is the workhorse. It's good and it's amazing how much you can lug around on a Pletscher rack, given an adequate number of bungee cords. (Please be careful when attaching and detaching bungee cords—they can put out an eye.) Two large bags of groceries are quite managable—be sure and get double-thickness bags, and be aware that a bike handles differently with that much weight on the rear.

A new West German rack, the ESGE, is both attractive and useful, but costs about three times as much as the Pletscher. Other more sophisticated racks, some lower in price than the ESGE, are sold with the touring cyclist's pannier bags in mind. An excellent model is sold by the Touring Cyclist Shop, Box 4009, Boulder, CO 80302.

It's impossible to adequately review all the brand-name handlebar, seat and pannier bags here. There are many good ones, in many useful configurations: handlebar bags, saddle bags, convertible backpack/panniers, frame triangle bags, and box- or roll-shaped bags that mount on the rear carrier. If you're commuting with a briefcase and lunch, don't bother with bags at all. Just supply yourself with bungee cords and a Pletscher rack. If you see the light and begin shopping by bike, first buy more bungee cords—they're cheap and you'll be shopping less anyway. If necessity requires it, try first the oblong "box" that sits on the rack and can be easily detached and taken along with you. Or, use common sense about mounting your own wooden box or homemade carrier.

LIGHTS

If you ride at all after dark, you must have head and tail lights, not reflectors. If you do a lot of night riding, it's worth the trouble to get the Soubitez "bloc" lamp/generator and replace the worthless headlight bulb with a larger, square model which throws an adequate beam. If your night mileage isn't great, use the Wonder Light, an excellent little flashlight/bike light that slips on and off the bike instantly. Headlights are at least 50% for the purpose of making you visible to others, but if your route demands good road surface visibility, mount two Wonder lights on the bars. By all means get two of the French leg lights. They're the greatest thing ever invented for night riding safety. Wear one above your left elbow and the other below the left knee. Beware the parallel-bar sewer grate while riding at night! We've seen them in the most unlikely places, including the middle of shopping center parking lots, where you're not looking for them. They can kill you.

ODDS & ENDS

Get the Bluemels plastic fenders—easy to mount in winter and take off in summer.

The IKU tire-drive speedometer is excellent. If you want to record only your total mileage, you can try a fork-attached velometer, though the tick-tick noise drives many cyclists batty.

The best rear view mirror is the little eyeglass-mounted wire-attached dentist's mirror. You can get one for $4.00 from Ultra-Light Touring Shop, Box 308, Brinkhaven, Ohio 43006. Be sure and tell them whether you'll be mounting the mirror on your cap bill, helmet, etc. If you'll be attaching it to eyeglass frames, specify whether your glasses have wide, thin, or wire temple pieces. Add 50 cents to your order if you want your name or other message engraved on the mirror.

BOOKS

For a very good listing of cycling books on repair, touring, racing, etc., write World Publications, Box 366, Mt. View, CA 94040. Frankly, they published the book you're now reading, but as active cyclists they sincerely try to stock only books which are of real use to the cyclist.

HELMETS

These were discussed earlier, but deserve to be touted once again. A cyclist recently came down a hill at over 30 mph near Bolinas, California. He was forced off the road by a wide camper trailer. There was a curb at the shoulder, and he went flying. His companions said he landed head first on the edge of the curb, then slid on the ground for about 60 feet. If he had not been wearing an MSR cycling helmet, he would certainly have died. This was one of the worst imaginable accidents—high speed, head striking a sharp edge. It's not surprising, therefore, that the helmet did break; but the cyclist lived to write a letter of appreciation to MSR for a helmet which saved his life.

You might think that around-town cycling is comparatively safe. On the contrary, country roads usually have soft shoulders for easier landings. It's safe to ride city streets if you know what you're doing, as we explained in an earlier chapter, but if you do go down, the hazards are great. Sharp curbs, hard road surfaces, hood ornaments and other steel edges are a few of the dangers. Get a helmet. The MSR and Bell models are the best. If you can't afford them, get a good hockey helmet.

LONG DISTANCE GEAR

If you're interested in specialized equipment for longer cycling trips, please consult the appendix of "Traveling By Bike," the best general reference on the subject (96 pp., paper-pack, illustrated, $1.95 from World Publications, Box 366, Mt. View, CA 94040.)

About the Author

Donald Pruden was born in 1934 in Paterson, New Jersey. He was educated at Rensselaer Polytechnic Institute, Syracuse University and the State University of New York, receiving a B.S. degree in biology and M.S. degrees in physics, math and science education. He has been a science and math teacher for 14 years and is currently on the faculty of the State University of New York at Albany, where he works as science and math supervisor at the Milne School, a teacher-training high school run by the university. He is married and has two children.

"I guess I've been on two wheels of some kind since second grade," Donald says. "My first 10-speed was a discount special which today I can look back on with some amusement—yet I loved it, too. Then, I saved every penny until I had enough for a Peugeot PX-10, which was purchased with bus fare saved by commuting on the discount special."

Donald has been teaching cycling classes for adults and high schoolers for several years now, and his students have dubbed him "The Orange Avenger," a title he's adopted with pride. The opposite of a sedentary academician, Pruden can frequently be found outdoors demonstrating the laws of physics that pertain to speed and acceleration by riding his bike from Robin St. to Lake Ave., in Albany, shooting marbles to demonstrate bicycle collision probability to math classes, racing a faculty colleague 20 miles down Route 85, or sharpening his fencing skills in the science department halls. A student wrote of her physics teacher, "If you don't know him, perhaps you think he is quiet and uninteresting, but he reveals himself as a fantastic, funny, reasonable, admirable but unbelievable man."

(Arnold LeFevre photo)